Anton Chekhov: Ivanov

adapted by David Hare

Anton Chekhov (1860–1904) first turned to writing as a medical student at Moscow University, from which he graduated in 1884. Among his early works were short monologues (*The Evils of Tobacco*), one-act farces (*The Bear*, *The Proposal*, *The Wedding*) and the extremely long *Platonov* material. His first completed full-length play was *Ivanov* (1887) followed by *The Wood Demon* (1889), *The Seagull* (1896), *Uncle Vanya* (1899), *Three Sisters* (1901) and *The Cherry Orchard* (1904).

David Hare was born in 1947 and educated at Lancing and Jesus College, Cambridge. His own work for the stage includes *Slag*, *The Great Exhibition*, *Brassneck* (with Howard Brenton), *Knuckle*, *Fanshen*, *Teeth 'n' Smiles*, *Plenty*, *A Map of the World*, *The Bay at Nice & Wrecked Eggs*, *Pravda* (with Howard Brenton), *Secret Rapture*, *Racing Demon*, *Murmuring Judges*, *The Absence of War*, *Skylight* and *Amy's View*. He has also adapted plays by Pirandello (*The Rules of the Game*) and Brecht (*The Life of Galileo* and *Mother Courage and her Children*).

PTO for label

also available

Bertolt Brecht
Mother Courage and her Children
(*version by David Hare*)

Chekhov Plays
The Cherry Orchard
Three Sisters
The Seagull
Uncle Vanya
and four vaudevilles
(*versions by Michael Frayn*)

KING ALFRED'S COLLEGE
WINCHESTER
891.72 /CHE
KA0209940X

for a complete catalogue of Methuen Drama write to:

Methuen Drama
Michelin House
81 Fulham Road
London SW3 6RB

Ivanov

A play in four acts by
Anton Chekhov

adapted by
David Hare

Methuen Drama

A Methuen Theatre Classic

This adaptation first published in Great Britain in 1997
by Methuen Drama
an imprint of Reed International Books Ltd
Michelin House, 81 Fulham Road, London SW3 6RB
and Auckland, Melbourne, Singapore and Toronto
and distributed in the United States of America
by Heinemann, a division of Reed Elsevier Inc.
361 Hanover Street, Portsmouth, New Hampshire
NH 03801-3959

Reprinted 1997

Adaptation copyright © 1997 by David Hare
Introduction copyright © 1997 by David Hare

The author has asserted his moral rights

ISBN 0 413 71050 5

A CIP catalogue record for this book is available from the British Library

Typeset by Wilmaset Ltd, Birkenhead, Wirral
Printed and bound in Great Britain
by Cox & Wyman Ltd, Reading, Berkshire

Caution
All rights in this adaptation are strictly reserved and application for performance etc should be made to Casarotto Ramsay, National House, 60–66 Wardour Street, London W1V 4ND. No performance may be given unless a licence has been obtained.

This paperback is sold subject to the condition that it shall not, by way of trade or otherwise, be lent, resold, hired out, or otherwise circulated without the publisher's prior consent in any form of binding or cover other than that in which it is published and without a similar condition being imposed on the subsequent purchaser.

Contents

Introduction

> I've tried to be original. I have not introduced a single villain or a single angel (though I haven't been able to abstain from fools); nor have I accused or vindicated anyone. Whether or not I've succeeded I can't tell. Korsh and the actors are sure the play will work. I'm not so sure. The actors don't understand it and say the most ridiculous things, they're badly miscast, I'm constantly at war with them. Had I known I'd never have got involved with it.
>
> Anton Chekhov

> How lonely Chekhov is. How little he's understood.
>
> Maxim Gorky

Because the Russian playwright Anton Chekhov (1860–1904) is known primarily through the four great masterpieces which have long been in the standard international repertory, it has become the practice to patronize his three earlier plays. Academics have been eager to treat them as if they are merely blueprints, the first stumblings of an apprentice towards a style which he was able to perfect only in the last nine years of his life. Perhaps we can allow that the absurdly long *Platonov* is indeed a sort of young man's mess. We can admit that *The Wood Demon* is only a sketch for the much more satisfying *Uncle Vanya*. But we are overlooking something really valuable if we regard the brilliant sport, the rogue play, *Ivanov*, simply as the staging-post of a writer on his way to greater things. It is hard not to feel that this drama of a Russian landowner's half-farcical, half-serious personal crisis would have been better understood had its author not gone on to develop quite different ambitions in his subsequent plays.

The slightly infuriating critical convention has been to claim that because *Ivanov* is a young play, it must necessarily be inferior. Chekhov was the man who later banished melodrama from the nineteenth-century stage, so it has become easy to forget the fact that he once wrote one exceptionally good melodrama himself. Because he tended to describe *Ivanov* so dismissively in his private correspondence, and because its early performances were so obviously inadequate, the author implicitly gave permission to successive commentators who have been only too ready to label it as clumsy. Originally drafted in only two weeks, the play uses monologue and direct address. It features a hero who makes conspicuously long speeches. It satirizes Russian society in much broader strokes than those Chekhov later favoured. But what entitles us to think these techniques are not deliberate, and, in their way, just as skilfully deployed as the more muted strategies Chekhov later adopted? Unless we can see that *Ivanov* is not a lesser play but simply *different* to the rest of his work, then we will miss the versatility of a playwright who can still surprise us by the variety of his styles, and, what's more, one whose special vigour and directness in this early extraordinary outing also cast light on the plays which follow.

Nothing has been more damaging to our feeling for Chekhov's plays than the way his admirers have tended to represent the author himself. Encouraged by suitably enigmatic photographs, we have tolerated the idea that he was in his own being some sort of all-purpose secular saint, a mythically detached human being who transported himself to a position approximately six feet above the rest of the human race, whence he was able to observe mankind's foibles with a medical man's detached and witty irony. Anyone who has bothered to establish the facts of Chekhov's life would find just how far off the mark this widely-accepted notion is. The real Chekhov was a considerably more complex, testier and troubled human being than his hagiographers make out. Indeed, to that tiresome school of academics who believe that literary criticism consists of marking off a writer's every line against a contemporary checklist of fashionable 'errors', the saintly Chekhov comes through with his halo looking distinctly askew.

When we hear this supposedly calm and virtuous playwright saying that when he entered a room full of good-looking young women he 'melted like a Yid contemplating his ducats', then we may begin to suspect that our man is not quite who he is commonly made out to be. When he is elsewhere quoted as observing that the most complimentary thing you can say about a woman is that 'she doesn't think like a woman'; when we discover him in Monte Carlo, fretfully revising an infallible system and then losing five hundred francs in two days; when we catch him referring to his one-time Jewish girlfriend as 'Efros the nose'; when we find him in Sri Lanka, in his own words, 'glutting himself on dusky women', then we are aleady thankfully waving goodbye to the floppy-hatted and languorous stereotype whose spirit pervades so many of our received ideas about the good doctor.

It is the singular virtue of the play *Ivanov* that it gives us our best sight of this more robust Chekhov, and one who is not frightened to use some quite orthodox dramatic conventions – each act climaxes with what he called 'a punch on the nose' – to tackle hotly contemporary themes. Here is a full-blooded writer, alive with passion and confusion, willing to address the ugliness of Russian anti-Semitism head-on, and dramatizing a conflict inside himself in a way which is both deeply felt and funny. If later the playwright's ideal becomes famously to hide himself as writer somewhere in the lattice-work of the play, so that you cannot detect the authorial voice in any of the characters, here, on the contrary, is a play where Chekhov's own thoughts and feelings are plainly on show.

It could hardly be otherwise. The dominating theme of *Ivanov* is honesty. It is hard to see how Chekhov could have written a play which asks what real honesty is, and – just as important – what its price is, without being willing to let a little more than usual of his own feelings to show. Although the play, like all his later work, may be said to weave together a whole variety of threads, nothing is more striking in it than the deliberate contrast between the self-confident Doctor Lvov and the more cautious Ivanov. The play's defining argument is between a young doctor who thinks that honesty is to do with blurting out offensive truths, and the more sensitive central character who insists, with a wisdom which is notably pre-Freudian, that no one can acquire honesty unless they also have the self-knowledge to examine their own motives.

In this debate there is no doubt with whom Chekhov's sympathies lie. 'If my Ivanov comes across as a blackguard or superfluous man and the doctor as a great man, if no one understands why Anna and Sasha love Ivanov, then my play has evidently failed, and there can be no question of having it produced.' Yet for all his protestations of partiality, Chekhov's achievement is to provide Ivanov with an opponent who is, in an odd way, as compelling as the hero, and almost at times his shadow. Chekhov leaves us to work out for ourselves whether honesty consists in judging others, or in refusing to judge them.

Apart from the charge of technical immaturity, the play has also had to survive the impression that, in Ivanov himself, it presents a hero who is excessively, even morbidly self-pitying. Yet, in saying this, critics wilfully ignore Chekhov's stated intention which was to kill off once and for all the strain of self-indulgent melancholy which he believed disfigured Russian literature. 'I have long cherished the audacious notion of summing up all that has hitherto been written about complaining and melancholy people, and would have my Ivanov proclaim the ultimate in such writing.' Far from idealizing the so-called superfluous man, Chekhov seeks to send him packing. In Ivanov he portrays a character who is actually horrified by the idea of depression, and who is repelled to find himself its victim. Far from indulging that melancholy – as perhaps some of the weaker characters in Chekhov's later plays do – Ivanov fights it. The play is the portrait of a man who will do anything rather than falsely dramatize his feelings. Viewed in this light, the play's tragic ending, which provided Chekhov with so much difficulty, seems to have a terrible logic.

But no summary of the play's themes can do justice to the sheer exuberance and vitality of Chekhov's youthful writing. In Anna and Sasha, here are two of his most affecting and convincing heroines; in Anna's final rejection of Ivanov, one of his greatest scenes. Here, in the two older men, Lebedev and Count Shabyelski, are two of his most touching portraits of people who know that their lives are going by too fast. Here also, in more detail than usual, and with more savagery, is the presentation of a whole society, trapped between social stagnation and a change it has no idea how to manage. *Ivanov* is a play with which Chekhov, for all his rewriting, never felt wholly satisfied. Yet as so often, there are ways in which a site of first literary struggles provides an infinitely richer experience for the audience than many a cooler, supposedly more mature play.

David Hare, 1997

Production History

Ivanov is the first play Chekhov actually completed. It was drafted in under two weeks in 1887. At the time Chekhov was known primarily as a comic short-story writer, and the play was commissioned by Korsh's theatre in Moscow which specialized in farce. The management was surprised by the seriousness of the play Chekhov delivered. There were few rehearsals. The production was shown in a double-bill with a French farce and the first night was famously unsatisfactory. According to the author, the actor playing Shabyelski got all his lines wrong in Act One. In Act Two the drunken party guests were indeed drunk. They improvised extensively, and some furniture was knocked over. Chekhov left, vowing never again to have anything to do with the theatre. The *New Times* commented 'No author of recent times has made his bow to such a hotch-potch of praise and protest.'

It was when the Alexandrine Theatre in St Petersburg wanted to present the play in 1889 that Chekhov began some serious rewriting, mainly of Acts Two and Four. In particular, he worked on the ending, which had never satisfied him. In spite of the author's own doubts, *Ivanov* this time played triumphantly, although it has never since joined his better-known plays in the world repertory.

Ivanov has an uneven record in Britain. Komisarjevsky directed the premiere in Barnes in 1925. John Gielgud played in his own production at the Phoenix Theatre in 1965, with Yvonne Mitchell as Anna and Clare Bloom as Sasha. The title role has since been taken by Derek Jacobi and John Wood. Most recently, Alan Bates appeared in Elijah Moshinsky's production at the Strand Theatre in 1989.

D.H.

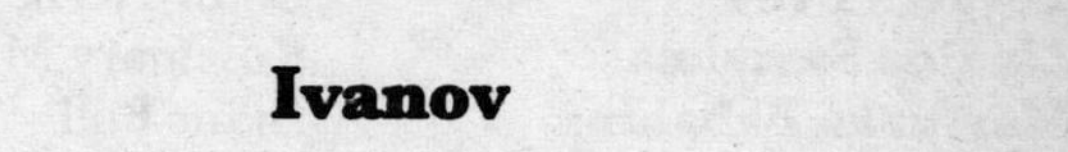

Ivanov

This adaptation of *Ivanov* was first performed at the Almeida Theatre, London, on 7 February 1997. The cast was as follows:

Nikolai Ivanov	Ralph Fiennes
Mikhail Borkin	Anthony O'Donnell
Anna Petrovna	Harriet Walter
Count Matvyei Shabyelski	Oliver Ford Davies
Yevgeni Lvov	Colin Tierney
Zinaida Savishna	Rosemary McHale
Marfusha Babakina	Diane Bull
Avdotya Nazarovna	Georgine Anderson
Kosykh	John Cater
Pavel Lebedev	Bill Paterson
Sasha	Justine Waddell
Gavrila	Sam Beazley
Pyotr	Richard Addison
First Guest	David Melville
Second Guest	Harry Gostelow
Third Guest	Richard Addison
Fourth Guest	Christopher Rickwood

Directed by Jonathan Kent
Designed by Tobias Hoheisel
Lighting by Mark Henderson
Music by Jonathan Dove
Sound by John A. Leonard

Characters

Nikolai Ivanov, *a regional councillor*
Mikhail Borkin, *the steward of Ivanov's estate*
Anna Petrovna, *Ivanov's wife, née Sarah Abramson*
Count Matvyei Shabyelski, *Ivanov's uncle*
Yevgeni Lvov, *a young country doctor*
Zinaida Savishna, *wife to Lebedev*
Marfusha Babakina, *a young widow and heiress*
Avdotya Nazarovna, *an old woman of no known profession*
Kosykh, *an excise officer*
Pavel Lebedev, *Chairman of the local council*
Sasha, *daughter to the Lebedevs, aged twenty*
Gavrila, *servant to the Lebedevs*
Pyotr, *servant to Ivanov*
First Guest
Second Guest
Third Guest
Fourth Guest
Other visitors, men and women

The action takes place in a province in Central Russia in the late 1880s.

This adaptation is based on a literal translation by Alex Wilbraham.

Characters

Nikolai Ivanov, a regional councillor
Mikhail Borkin, a distant relative and manager of his estate
Anna Petrovna, Ivanov's wife, née Sarah Abramson
Count Matvei Shabelsky, Ivanov's uncle
Yevgeni Lvov, a young country doctor
Zinaida Savishna, Lebedev's wife
Marfa Babakina, a young widow
Avdotya Nazarovna, an old woman of no fixed employment
Kosykh, an excise officer
Pavel Lebedev, Chairman of the local council
Sasha, daughter of the Lebedevs, aged twenty
Gavrila, servant to the Lebedevs
Pyotr, Ivanov's servant
First Guest
Second Guest
Third Guest
Fourth Guest
Other guests and servants

The action takes place in a province in Central Russia in the late 1880s.

This adaptation is based on a literal translation by Alexa... Vill...

Act One

The garden of **Ivanov**'*s estate. On the left is the façade of a house with a terrace. One window is open. In front of the terrace is a wide semi-circular area, from which paths lead to the right and straight ahead. On the right-hand side there are small benches, tables and chairs. On one table a lamp is already lit. Evening is drawing in. As the curtain rises, the sound of a duet for cello and piano, coming from indoors.*

1

Ivanov *is sitting at the table reading a book.* **Borkin**, *the steward, appears from the depths of the garden, in big boots and carrying a gun. He is high on drink. He goes quietly up to* **Ivanov**, *and when he is near aims the gun at his head.* **Ivanov** *jumps up.*

Ivanov My God, what on earth are you doing?

Borkin (*very quietly*) Bang!

Ivanov Misha, honestly, you know what my life's like . . .

Borkin (*laughing*) I know, I do know . . .

Ivanov Why do you do it? Why do you do these things?

Borkin (*conceding*) All right I promise . . .

Ivanov You seem to get some sort of pleasure . . .

Borkin . . . I'll never shoot you again.

Ivanov Thank you. I'm trying to read.

Ivanov *has sat down again.* **Borkin** *sits down beside him and takes off his cap.*

Borkin My God, it's so hot. You wouldn't believe it. I've covered fifteen miles in under three hours. I'm exhausted. Feel.

Ivanov Later.

Borkin Come on, feel. Here.

He has taken **Ivanov**'*s hand and put it on his chest.*

An irregular beat. There. Boom-boom-boom-*boom*. It's a murmur of the heart. I could drop dead any moment. Then what would you feel?

Ivanov I'd feel nothing.

Borkin No, really. I'm asking. Tell me.

Ivanov I'd feel I could finish my book.

Borkin Sweet fellow, I really am asking. Tell me the truth: would you be upset?

Ivanov Only one thing upsets me. The smell of stale vodka.

Borkin You can smell vodka? Amazing. Or maybe not, after all. In Plesniki I ran into the presiding judge. Do you know him? We had eight glasses each. What a great judge! Though if you ask my opinion, drinking is bad for you. In the long run. That's my opinion. Drinking is harmful. What's your view?

Ivanov Oh for God's sake, this is unbearable. Do you have no idea of what this is like?

Borkin I plead guilty, your honour.

He gets up to go.

Please. Sit alone. Such cultured people! You're not even allowed to speak to them.

He turns back.

Oh, just one thing. I need the eighty-two roubles.

Ivanov What eighty-two roubles?

Borkin Tomorrow. (*Reminding him.*) The workmen? The roubles?

Ivanov I don't have it.

Borkin Oh, well, thank you. I'll tell them that, then. That's marvellous. Let me rehearse. 'I don't have it.' How was that?

Ivanov I have no money. Wait till the end of the month. That's when the council pays me.

Borkin You tell them. You go and tell them. I'd love to hear you. 'I don't have any money. The council hasn't paid me yet'! I'd love to hear you tell them that!

Ivanov What do you want me to do? There's no point in asking me. What is this? What on earth is the point?

Borkin What is it? What *is* it?

They are beginning to lose their tempers.

It's me asking when we're going to pay our own workers. Call yourself a landowner? Oh yes, 'progressive farming techniques'! May I remind you: you control a thousand acres of land, and yet you don't have a rouble in your pocket. It's like owning a cellar full of wine and losing the corkscrew. What am I meant to do? I'll take the troika tomorrow and sell the wretched thing. Why not? I sold the oats before they'd even been harvested. Tomorrow I may as well sell the corn. It's fine. Do you think it bothers me? Ay-ay-ay! If you're looking for someone who gets bothered, you've come to the wrong man.

2

Borkin *has begun to pace up and down. Now the voice of* **Count Shabyelski** *comes from indoors.*

Shabyelski (*off*) You're impossible to play with. Your touch is appalling, and you've got the ear of a fish!

At once, **Ivanov**'*s wife,* **Anna Petrovna** *appears at the open window.*

Anna What's going on? Misha? Why all this stamping about?

Borkin Tell me how you live with your darling Nikolai and manage to not stamp about.

Anna I meant to ask, can we have some hay put on the croquet lawn?

Borkin Oh, just . . . leave me alone!

Anna Well, really. What a tone to use to a woman! And when I gather you're so keen to attract one as well!

She turns cheerfully to **Ivanov**.

Shall we go and turn cartwheels out there in the hay, my darling?

Ivanov Anna, you know the cold air is bad for you. Please go back in. (*Shouts.*) Uncle, can you close it? Please!

The window is closed.

Borkin We have only two days left to pay Lebedev his interest.

Ivanov (*looks at his watch*) That's why I have to go there tonight.

Borkin Of course, I'd forgotten, that's right, it's his daughter's birthday . . .

Ivanov I shall go and ask him to be patient.

Borkin Hey, it's Sasha's birthday. Why don't I come with you?

He sings and does a little dance.

'If you're coming, I'm going; if you're going, I'm coming . . .' (*Speaks.*) I'll have a quick swim. Chew a little blotting paper, then rinse my mouth out with meths and I can start drinking all over again. The sad thing is, you don't realize just how much I love you, my friend. You're always so moody, you find life so lowering. But you never look round and think 'At least I've got a friend.' I'd do anything for you. I could even marry Marfusha Babakina. Yes. She's a dumb bitch but I'd do it. You could have half the dowry. Dammit, you could have the whole thing.

Ivanov You do talk such nonsense.

Borkin But that's where you're wrong. (*Imitates him.*) 'You do talk such nonsense.' Why? Why is that nonsense? If that's what you wanted, that's what I'd do. I'm serious! It's a shame, you're such a bright man, so brilliant, but where is the whatsit? That little bit of extra? You know what I'm saying? Where is the drive? If you could only . . . I don't know . . . make the big gesture. If you were a normal person I could make you a million a year. Look, for example, say I was you – I'm you, all right? – if I had two thousand roubles today, then I swear within two weeks, I'd have twenty thousand. In the hand! There you go, look, your lips moving already: 'It's nonsense!' But it isn't nonsense, it's so! On the opposite riverbank Ovsianov is selling his holding. If we bought that strip of land, then both of the banks would be ours. And then . . . well, you can imagine . . . we'd start saying we had plans for a mill. And for a mill we'd need to build a dam. And then we'd say to everyone who's living downriver and who obviously would hate the idea: 'All right, if you don't want it, I'm sorry, *meine Damen und Herren*, but we're going to build it unless you pay up.' The Zarevsky factory would give us five thousand, Korolkov three thousand, the monastery would be good for six . . .

Ivanov Misha, please, I don't want an argument. I will not listen to these schemes of yours.

3

Count Shabyelski *comes out of the house with* **Doctor Lvov** *who is twenty-six.*

Shabyelski Doctors and lawyers, there's really no difference except lawyers just rob you, doctors rob you and kill you as well.

Borkin (*sitting at the table*) Oh of course, it's not just that you won't do anything. But I'm not allowed to do anything either!

Shabyelski *sits on the little bench.*

Shabyelski Present company excepted, of course. Every one of them charlatans. Frauds. Perhaps in Utopia there exists an honest doctor. But as a man who has spent twenty thousand on medicine in his life, I can say: I've never met one who wasn't an obvious quack.

Borkin Enterprise, of course, that's vulgar. Not enough for *you* not to have any, but none of the rest of us must have any either.

Shabyelski Present company excepted, I have said. There may be other exceptions. But.

He yawns. **Ivanov** *shuts his book and addresses* **Lvov**.

Ivanov Well?

Lvov As I said this morning, she must go to the Crimea, and at once.

He has glanced at the window and is now pacing up and down. **Shabyelski** *snorts.*

Shabyelski The Crimea! Why, Misha, you and I must try this doctoring racket. As soon as some bubble-headed housewife starts clearing her throat, then out with the scientific prescription: off to the Crimea! And then no doubt, when she gets there, the regular attentions of some virile young brute.

Ivanov In the name of God, Uncle, will you stop talking such tripe?

He turns back to **Lvov**.

She won't go. Even if I could raise the money – which I can't – she'll still refuse.

Lvov Yes. As things are.

There is a pause.

Borkin I mean what are we saying here? Just how ill is she? Does she really have to go all that way?

Lvov (*glancing again at the window*) Yes. It's tuberculosis.

Borkin Ah, well then. I must say. Fair enough. Lately whenever I've looked at her, I have thought 'She's not with us long.'

Lvov Please. Quietly. She can hear you in there.

There is a pause.

Borkin That's life. What is it? A flower. It blossoms, it blooms. Then a goat comes along. Sk-lumph. And it's gone.

Shabyelski It's nonsense, she's fine. (*Yawns.*) Charlatans merely. And frauds.

There is a pause.

Borkin Now what I've been doing is trying to teach Nikolai here ways to make money. I had a brilliant idea. But Nikolai is not interested. Why not? Because Nikolai is gloomy. He's jaundiced. He's woebegone. Nikolai is forlorn. How is Nikolai? He's down in the dumps.

Shabyelski (*getting up and stretching*) Oh, you're such an entrepreneur. You're so full of advice for everyone, but you never have any for me.

Borkin I'm going for a swim.

Shabyelski Why don't you help me?

Borkin Goodbye to you all!

Shabyelski I mean it. Instruct me! Give me lessons: how to get ahead!

Borkin If you're really interested, you could be up twenty thousand by the end of the week.

Shabyelski Well then, show me!

Borkin I guarantee it.

Shabyelski Teach me!

Borkin Nikolai, by the way, lend me a rouble, will you?

Ivanov *silently gives* **Borkin** *a rouble.* **Shabyelski** *has got up to pursue him.*

Borkin Thank you. There's nothing to it. It's simple.

Shabyelski But what do I actually do?

Borkin I promise: twenty thousand, thirty thousand, how much do you want?

They go out. **Ivanov** *and* **Lvov** *are silent for a moment.*

Ivanov Needless words. Needless people. A perpetual drizzle of stupid questions. All this, Doctor, has exhausted me to the point of sickness. I am so angry I no longer know who I am. For whole days I'm driven mad by an unceasing noise in my head. I can't sleep and my ears buzz. But where can I put myself? Truly?

Lvov Nikolai Alekseyevich, we need a serious talk.

Ivanov By all means.

Lvov You say Anna will not go, but she will go if you accompany her.

Ivanov Yes. But it would cost twice as much. Also, I've already had leave from work. I can't ask again.

Lvov Then listen. Whether she goes or not, what Anna needs above all is peace. She needs quiet. But every moment of the day Anna is in torment. The only thing she cares about is you, and your feelings towards her. Forgive me. But by your behaviour you are killing her.

There is a pause.

Ivanov, I want to think well of you. I want to believe in you.

Ivanov Yes, it's true, I know. I'm sure it's all my fault. You're right. But I'm confused, I'm . . . what? I'm *possessed*, is that right? Is that the right word? How do I put this? I lack strength. That's it. I lack the strength to lift myself up. The fact is, I've ceased to understand anyone, anything.

He glances at the window.

My friend, if you want, I can tell you the whole story, but . . . not here. We'll walk. I'll give you an inkling. Yes? A sketch. Anna . . . now, if we start with Anna . . . we agree, she's a wonderful woman. An extraordinary woman. Any sacrifice I required, she was ready to make. For my sake, she forsook her religion, she abandoned her parents, she gave up all prospect of wealth. She gave up the name she was born with. Whereas I . . . as you know, I am in no sense wonderful. On my side, I have sacrificed precisely nothing. I married her because I loved her passionately and I swore to love her for ever but . . . all right. Guess! Five years have gone by, she is still in love, and I . . .

He spreads his hands to finish.

You tell me she's going to die, and I feel not love, nor even pity, but just a terrible kind of emptiness. I'm sure from the outside – I accept this – it must seem shocking.

4

Ivanov *and* **Lvov** *walk off towards the avenue, as* **Shabyelski** *comes in, roaring with laughter.*

Shabyelski My God, this man isn't a fraud, he's a genius . . .

Ivanov (*going out*) But I am past the stage where I can make sense of it.

Shabyelski He's part-lawyer, part-accountant and part-doctor. In other words, all the most poisonous modern professions rolled into one.

He sits on the bottom step of the terrace.

Shame he never finished his studies. Give him a liberal education, with just that extra little bit of culture, and you'd have the perfect con man. 'No problem' he says 'You can make twenty thousand by the end of the week. Just trade in your assets. Trade your title' he says . . .

He laughs. **Anna** *opens the window.*

Next question is 'Why don't I fix you up with Marfusha?' he asks. *Qui ça?* Marfusha Babakina, of course. The one with a nose like a cab-driver. Oh yes, ideal countess material.

Anna Is that you, Count?

Shabyelski Who's that?

Anna *is laughing.*

Shabyelski (*in a Jewish accent*) What's so funny, my dear?

Anna Something you said at dinner once. How does it go? A horse, a what, a Jew?

Shabyelski
'A horse you once saw limping
A thief who claims he's cured
A Jew who says he's Christian –
And you'd better be insured.'

Anna *laughs again.*

Anna The simplest joke and of course it has to be malicious. No, I'm serious. I hadn't realized until recently how much it affects me. It does. Living with you, just being with you, Count, is depressing. Because in your eyes everyone is a phoney or a crook. Tell me, in honesty, do you have a good word for anyone?

Shabyelski What a question!

Anna I mean it. You and I have lived under the same roof for five years and not once have I heard you praise a single human being. Why? What have they all done to you? Do you think yourself so much better?

Shabyelski Far from it. If I'm hard on others, my God, I'm hardest of all on myself. What have I become? A parasite. Years ago, I was free, I was rich, I was happy, even. Now, what am I? I'm the licensed buffoon. Whatever I say, it makes no difference. I can be as rude as I like, they just think 'The old man's off his head.' They pay no attention.

Anna (*quietly*) It's screeching again.

Shabyelski Screeching?

Anna The owl. Every night it screeches.

Shabyelski Let it screech. Things can't get worse than they are already.

He stretches himself.

Oh, Anna, if I could just win that lottery, a small win, not even a big one, the things I could do! The places I'd show you! I'd be off your hands and not be back in this house till Judgement Day.

Anna Where would you go first?

Shabyelski Oh. Moscow. To hear the famous gypsy choir. Then on to Paris. I'd rent a flat, go to the Russian church.

Anna And what else?

Shabyelski I'd sit by my wife's grave for days. I'd sit, just thinking. And waiting for death. My wife is buried in Paris.

Anna Buried?

There is a pause.

How depressing! Can we play some more music?

Shabyelski Of course. Set it up.

5

Anna *goes back indoors.* **Ivanov** *and* **Lvov** *reappear from their walk.*

Ivanov My friend, you only graduated last year. You're young and full of life. I'm thirty-five. So I'm perfectly placed to offer you advice. It's this: don't marry a blue-stocking, an hysteric or a Jew. You think I'm joking, but I'm not. On the contrary. My advice would be: go for someone ordinary. The less stimulation the better. Get into a routine. I mean it. Finally it's safer. It's like, strong colours are fun, but ultimately it's cleverer to wear grey. What I'm saying is: don't take on the world. Don't tilt at windmills. Don't waste your time bashing your head against brick walls. What that means is, at least in my experience, at all costs stay away from progressive farming. Yes. And progressive education. And most of all, God help us! progressive rhetoric. It's a killer. Just pull your little shell up over your head, and get on with your life. Finally, it's the only way. I did the other thing, and it has destroyed me. I cannot tell you. My life? A story of unceasing error and absurdity!

He suddenly sees **Shabyelski**.

Oh Uncle, I cannot believe it!

Shabyelski What?

Ivanov Am I never to be alone?

He has blurted this out and **Shabyelski** *is hurt.*

Shabyelski And I . . . and *I*?

Ivanov Oh God!

Shabyelski I suppose I have nowhere.

Ivanov No! No, for God's sake!

Shabyelski I am always in the way, I am not to exist!

He jumps up and goes into the house. **Ivanov** *at once shouts after him.*

Ivanov Oh Lord, I'm sorry. Uncle, I'm sorry!

He turns back to **Lvov**.

What am I doing? What have I done?

Lvov Nikolai . . .

Ivanov How could I offend him like that? It's unforgivable. I must stop this. I must.

Lvov Nikolai, I have to speak frankly.

Ivanov *looks at him a moment.*

Ivanov Very well.

Lvov I must tell you the truth.

Ivanov The truth? Go ahead.

Lvov I have listened, I have tried to listen as best I may. But it seems to me you cannot speak, no, you cannot even open your mouth without talking about yourself. Always. The subject is 'I'. It is 'I'! Just fifteen feet away – my God, the selfishness of it, the heartlessness – a woman is dying. She is dying from her very love for you. Her time on this earth is coming to an end. And yet you prance around like a pigeon boasting of your own . . . what do you call it? Despair! Words . . . the words are not in my gift, but I can only say: you are a man who is detestable.

Ivanov Perhaps. You see me from the outside. Probably you're right.

He listens a moment.

It sounds as if the horses are ready. I must go and change.

He stops on his way back into the house.

You do not hide your feelings, Doctor. You do not like me, and you say so. I admire you for that.

He goes inside. **Lvov** *is alone.*

Lvov I cannot believe it. What is it? What is it that stops me from speaking? I begin to confront him and my chest clamps. My tongue sticks to the roof of my mouth. How could I have let that moment go by? That was my moment. How I hate him. This impostor, this over-educated Tartuffe! He is going out! Going out, when his wife's only hope of happiness is when he is close. He is her life. She begs him, implores him to stay just one evening at home. And he . . . cannot. Home? Not interesting enough. An evening at home and he'd have to shoot himself. Of course. This man needs space. He needs air. He needs room to think up new ways to betray her. I know why you go to visit the Lebedevs! I know!

6

Shabyelski *comes out of the house with* **Anna** *and* **Ivanov** *who is now wearing a coat and hat.*

Shabyelski Nikolai, it's not right, it's completely unfair. You go out every night and we stay at home. We go to bed at eight from sheer boredom. Do you call this life? You're allowed out and we're not?

Anna Count, leave him alone. Let him go.

Ivanov Yes, but what about you, my dear sweet invalid? Ask the doctor. You shouldn't be out at this hour. You're not a child, Anna.

Anna No.

Ivanov You must think.

Anna Yes.

There is a moment's pause.

Of course.

Ivanov (*to* **Shabyelski**) Why are you so desperate to come with me?

Shabyelski To be anywhere! Not to be here! You make me stay at home, so that Anna will not be bored, you say, but it seems not to occur to you that you are leaving your wife in the company of the most boring person on earth.

Anna Leave him, Count. Let him go. He likes it there.

Ivanov Anna, I am hardly going because I 'like' it. I am not going because I like it. I am going because I have to discuss my debts.

Anna You don't have to justify yourself. Just go. Who is keeping you?

Ivanov Everyone, please let's . . . let's please be pleasant to one another.

Shabyelski Nikolai, I beg you. I haven't been out since Easter. I need people I can despise, I need entertainment.

Ivanov All right, very well. My God, how you bore me!

Shabyelski *takes his arm to thank him.*

Shabyelski Oh thank you, thank you. God in heaven be praised. But your hat, Nikolai, the straw one . . . may I borrow it?

Ivanov You can. Only quickly. Please!

Shabyelski *runs into the house.*

Ivanov How did this happen? How did I reach this point?

He at once realizes what he has said.

Oh Lord, I'm sorry, how can I say such things? Anna, I'm sorry. I am not myself, this is not how I speak. This is not me. And now goodbye, I'll be back about one.

Anna My darling, please.

Ivanov What? My sweet one, my darling.

There is a pause.

Anna Please stay.

Ivanov Anna, my sweet one, my own, I do have to ask you, please don't stop me. Don't stop me going out. I know it's selfish, but, forgive me, I need this selfishness. It must be allowed. As soon as the sun goes down, my own home begins to oppress me. I become consumed with anguish. Why? If only I knew! I feel terrible here, I go to the Lebedevs', I feel worse. I come home, I feel worse still. And so it goes. I am desperate.

Anna Nikolai, why not stay? We'll talk. We'll talk as we once talked. Let's eat together and read. That old Misery and I have learnt all this music. We've learnt it for you.

She puts her arms round him.

Stay!

There is a pause.

I don't understand. It's been a year now. What changed you?

Ivanov I don't know. I don't know.

Anna Then why can't I come? Why can't I come visiting with you?

Ivanov All right, let me say it. You ask me a question, I will tell you, since we value the truth. When I am in this state, I begin not to love you. Yes. That's why I run. When I do not love you, I have to get out of the house.

Anna I understand. I understand this anguish. I understand it. Try, why not? Try to sing. Try to laugh. Anything. Get angry. I don't mind. Just stay. Have a drink. Laugh. Shout. We'll drive your anguish away. I'll sing for you. We'll lie in the hay. We'll sit in the study, in the dark, as we once sat in the dark, and you can talk about your unhappiness. Your eyes are so full of suffering. I shall look into them and cry, and we'll both feel better.

She begins to laugh and cry.

How does it go, that song? 'The flowers return in spring, but not the joy.' That's it, isn't it? Well then, go.

Ivanov Pray for me, Anna.

He starts to go out, then stops for a moment and thinks.

I can't stay! I can't!

He goes out. **Anna** *sits at the table.*

Anna Then go.

Lvov *continues to pace.*

Lvov Anna Petrovna, you must make a rule: on the dot of six you must go indoors and not come out till sunrise. The damp in the evening is bad for you.

Anna Whatever you wish, monsieur.

Lvov Why do you say that? Why do you talk like that? I'm serious.

Anna But I don't want to be serious.

She starts to cough.

Lvov There, I told you. You've begun to cough.

7

Shabyelski *comes out of the house in a hat and jacket. He hurries across to kiss* **Anna***'s hand.*

Shabyelski Where's Nikolai? Are the horses waiting? Good night to you, my beautiful. (*Pulling a face.*) Mazeltov and e-schkoozer me.

He goes out quickly.

Lvov Very funny.

There is a pause. The sound of an accordion in the distance.

Anna It's so unfair. The cooks, the coachmen, they get to dance. And I? I never dance. Yevgeni Konstantinovich, why are you pacing about? Come and sit down.

Lvov I can't.

There is a pause.

Anna They're playing 'The Starling' in the kitchen. (*Sings.*)
'Starling, starling, where have you been?
Drinking vodka on the green . . .'

There is a pause.

Are your parents still alive, Doctor?

Lvov My father died. My mother's still living.

Anna Do you miss her?

Lvov Oh well, you know. I'm so busy.

Anna (*laughs*) 'The flowers return in spring, but not the joy . . .' Who taught me that? I've forgotten. It must have been him.

She listens.

The owl again.

Lvov Let it bloody well screech.

Anna I suppose I'm beginning to feel, Doctor, that life has somehow short-changed me. Most people, perhaps no more deserving than me, are happy. They pay nothing for their happiness. But I have paid. I am paying with my whole life. Why is such high interest demanded of me?

She looks at him a moment.

What did you say?

Lvov I didn't say anything.

Anna You are always so kind to me, so considerate. Do you think I haven't guessed what is wrong with me? I know perfectly well. It's boring to talk about. (*With a Jewish accent.*) Mazeltov and e-schkoozer me. How are you on funny stories?

Lvov Hopeless. I can't tell them.

Anna He does. Brilliantly. And also I begin to be shocked at the cruelty of people. Why is love not answered with love? Why is truth always answered with lies? Tell me, how long are my own mother and father going to go on hating me? From fifty miles away, day and night, even in my sleep, I can feel their hatred. How am I to deal with my husband? He says it's only in the evening, he stops loving me only in the evening, when the anguish is at its worst. I see that. But during the day . . . Say he stopped loving me entirely. Of course it's not possible. But if he did? If he has? No. Don't think about it. (*Sings.*)
'Starling, starling, where have you been . . .'

She shudders.

How frightened I am! You've never married, Doctor, you understand nothing.

He sits down beside her.

Lvov You say you are shocked, Anna. No, it is I who am shocked. You are so clever, so upright, so honest. How did you end up in this place? What do you have in common with that unfeeling husband . . . all right, I'll leave him out of it . . . but why do you go on living in these depraved surroundings? That mad, mumbling, lunatic Count! And

Borkin, that appalling plug-ugly little thug. Explain to me. What are you doing? Why on earth do you stay?

Anna You sound like him. It's funny. Him as he used to be. His eyes used to grow round. When he talked, they glowed like burning coals. He blazed with passion. Go on, talk to me more!

Lvov *gets up, waving a hand.*

Lvov Talk? Why? What's the point?

He suddenly shouts.

Just go indoors!

Anna You are so confident. My husband is this. My husband is that. But how can you tell? You haven't even known him six months. This man was remarkable. Two years ago. Or three. There was no man ever like him. I saw him once, *once* across a room. It's true. I saw him and the trap was sprung. I met him, I loved him at sight. He said 'follow me', I followed. My life died behind me. It died, I killed it, quite consciously I killed it, and I never looked back.

There is a pause.

It's only now . . . only now when he goes to the Lebedevs' to be with other women. While I sit in the garden and the owl screeches.

A watchman is heard, knocking against the fences to drive away thieves.

And you don't have any brothers? Sisters?

Lvov None.

She cries.

Tell me. Tell me what's happening.

Anna (*stands*) I can't stand it. I am going there.

Lvov What do you mean?

Anna I shall follow him. I am going to find him. Order up the horses. Bring me the horses, quick!

She runs into the house.

Lvov No, this is not it. This is unprofessional. Not only do they fail to pay me, but they rip my heart out as well. Enough! I withdraw my services.

He goes into the house.

Act Two

A reception room at the Lebedevs' house. In the middle a door gives onto the garden, and there are doors to left and right. There is a great deal of expensive furniture, but the chandeliers, candelabras and pictures are under dust-sheets.

1

A game of cards is going on at the back of the stage. Among the players are **Kosykh**, *the excise officer and* **Avdotya Nazarovna**, *an old woman. Throughout the act guests are seen coming and going through the garden and the room.* **Gavrila**, *their servant, is in attendance.*

The young widow and heiress **Marfusha Babakina** *comes in, and heads straight for* **Lebedev**'*s wife,* **Zinaida Savishna** *who is on the sofa. Around her young men are sitting on stiff-backed chairs.*

Zinaida My darling Marfusha, how wonderful to see you.

Babakina Congratulations, my dear, on your daughter's birthday.

They kiss.

May God give her everything she desires.

Zinaida We thank you. We are simply so happy. And tell us, how have you been?

Babakina I've been well. Greetings, young friends.

The women sit together on the sofa. The men get up and bow.

First Guest Young? Come now, I suppose you're going to start claiming to be old.

Babakina I could hardly still hope to call myself young.

First Guest Please. It is only in name that you are a widow, Babakina. You are more attractive than any young girl.

There is a moment's pause. **Gavrila** *has brought* **Babakina** *tea.*

Zinaida Why on earth are you serving the tea without sweetening, Gavrila? Tea is nothing without jam. Some gooseberry, perhaps.

Babakina No. No thank you. No gooseberry.

Zinaida Are you sure?

Babakina Thanks but no thanks all the same.

There is another moment.

First Guest So. Tell us, Marfusha Babakina. How did you get here?

Babakina How?

First Guest Yes. By what route?

Babakina Oh . . .

First Guest Did you come through Muschkino?

Babakina No. I took the Zaimischche road. It's quicker.

First Guest Good thinking.

Kosykh Two spades.

Second Guest Pass.

Fourth Guest Pass.

Avdotya Pass.

Babakina And what about the price of the lottery tickets?

Zinaida Oh, don't tell us, we know!

Babakina Two-seventy roubles to enter the first draw. For the second, I do not exaggerate, already two-fifty. It's unprecedented.

Zinaida Just think, those fortunate souls who have already invested.

Babakina You say that, but the fact is, there's no guarantee.

Zinaida Yes, but what you're buying is hope. (*Sighs.*) Who knows? It's a ticket. God may be kind.

Third Guest You raise an interesting point. Is one well off with capital at all at this time? Look at interest rates. Dividends have gone through the floor. One is bound to ask is one better off with one's capital invested or with . . . or with . . . or with, well, its opposite . . .

Babakina Capital not invested?

Third Guest That's right.

The **First Guest** *yawns.*

Babakina And now one may yawn in front of ladies?

First Guest I'm sorry. I forgot myself.

Zinaida *gets up and goes out of the room. A silence.*

Fourth Guest Two diamonds.

Avdotya Pass.

Second Guest Pass.

Kosykh Pass.

Babakina Lord Jesus, the tedium. It is as if one had actually died.

2

Now **Zinaida** *is heard talking under her breath to her husband* **Lebedev** *as she leads him into the room.*

Zinaida What a prima donna! What on earth were you doing, sitting out here? These are your guests. You must mingle.

Lebedev Oh God, what an unendurable life we do lead.

Zinaida *has resumed her place.* **Lebedev** *now sees* **Babakina**.

Lebedev But look who's here. Radiance, beauty and laughter, sitting among us. (*Greeting her.*) How are you, you gorgeous piece of nougat?

Babakina Happy to be here.

Lebedev And we are happy to have you. Happy. Happy.

He sits down in an armchair.

So. Very well. I could do with a vodka.

He drinks the vodka **Gavrila** *serves him in one, then has a glass of water.*

First Guest Your good health, sir.

Lebedev Health? I'm alive, that's all one can say.

He turns to his wife.

And where has the birthday girl got to, my love?

Kosykh (*tearful*) I just don't understand it. We haven't won anything. I simply . . . I cannot believe it. Not one. Not one single trick.

He has jumped up in despair, and now **Avdotya Nazarovna** *gets up also, furious.*

Avdotya Whose fault is that? For goodness' sake you went into their suits.

Kosykh I didn't!

Avdotya No wonder you were left with the ace.

Kosykh That is simply not true. Let me tell you . . . everyone, I'll tell you my hand.

Lebedev Please!

Kosykh In diamonds, no, listen, I am holding, the king, the queen and the jack. I also have the eight. I have the ace of spades. Yet she – can you believe this? – she refuses my slam.

Avdotya I didn't.

Kosykh I bid no trumps . . .

Avdotya What do you mean? I bid no trumps. It was you who bid two!

Kosykh (*to* **Lebedev**) Dear friend, I implore you. I ask you to judge this. Let me recap, my diamonds are as follows . . .

Lebedev (*holding his ears*) Will somebody please get this man to stop?

Avdotya It was me! As God is my witness. It was me who bid the no trumps!

Kosykh For as long as I breathe on this planet, I will never again play cards with this flabby old trout!

Kosykh *runs into the garden.*

Avdotya Trout! How dare he? The man has no conception of manners.

Babakina My dear Avdotya, you seem to have mislaid your manners yourself.

Avdotya *now sees* **Babakina** *and throws open her arms.*

Avdotya Oh forgive me, my little plum, my angel, Babakina. Here I am, it's true, I'm talking like a fool. I didn't even see you, my lollipop.

She kisses her on the shoulder and sits down next to her.

Let me look at you, gorgeous. Perfection! But I mustn't praise you too highly, or it'll bring you bad luck.

Lebedev Praise her all you like, she still needs a husband.

Avdotya A husband? I promise you, my darling, finding you and Sasha husbands will be my life's work.

She gestures across the room.

Though goodness knows where from, to judge by the present selection. Look at them, sitting there, like hens in the rain.

Third Guest That hardly seems a suitable comparison. Have you thought, perhaps there's a good reason why men are now choosing to stay single? Surely it says something about the society in which we now live?

Lebedev Oh please, anything but social theory. Spare us. Life is too short.

3

Sasha *comes in and goes straight to her father.*

Sasha Such a beautiful evening, and you're all sitting here in this fug!

Zinaida Sasha, did you not notice Marfusha Babakina is present?

Sasha I apologize. I didn't see you.

Babakina Really, Sasha, you've got so stand-offish, you no longer come and see me at all.

They kiss, then **Sasha** *sits down next to her father.*

Congratulations.

Sasha Well thank you.

Lebedev No question you're right, Avdotya, there's a shortage of decent prospects. Forget would-be bridegrooms, you can't even find a best man. Young men today, they're all insipid. Cheerless. They don't know how to dance, they can't articulate, they can't even drink.

Avdotya I'd say drink is the one thing they can do.

Lebedev I don't mean drink like a horse drinks. I mean drink like we used to. After a hard day at lectures, at study, then out with the ladies, drinking and dancing till dawn. And talking! Talking like men kissed by the Almighty, talking with the eloquence of gods. But now . . .

He gestures dismissively.

You look, you see only dishmops. Men who are halfway to women, it seems. There's only one real man in the district. Needless to say he's already married. Oh yes, and one other small detail: he's also gone off his head.

Babakina Who can you mean?

Lebedev Well, naturally I'm talking about Ivanov.

Babakina Ah yes. A good man. But look at him: desperately unhappy.

Zinaida Well, is it any surprise?

Babakina (*sighs*) Ah well . . .

Zinaida It's his own fault. How could he? What an obvious disaster. Marrying a Jew. And as usual, it doesn't pay off. All he wanted was to get his hands on little Sarah Abramson's fortune. But the parents were ahead of him. They cut her off, the day she changed her religion. As soon as she changed her name. He should have foreseen it. But now the poor man's lumbered.

Sasha Mother, that is simply not true.

Babakina Oh my dear, I think one may say it's commonly accepted.

Sasha Is it?

Babakina It is pretty obvious. Why else would anyone marry a Jew? Are you telling me there aren't enough nice Russian girls?

She is becoming extremely animated.

The sad thing is, it's not him that suffers. She does. He's so cruel, he's always angry because he knows he made a mistake. He comes home, he shouts 'It's your fault, your parents have swindled me.' People have heard him. 'Get out of my house!' But where can she go? Her family's disowned her. I suppose she could work as a maid. At a pinch. If she trained. Her life is just torture. If it weren't for the presence of his uncle, why, I believe Ivanov could well have murdered her.

Avdotya I've heard he did throw her in the cellar one time.

Babakina I've heard that.

Avdotya The best bit: he forced her to eat garlic.

Babakina It was garlic?

Avdotya I'm sure. It's a fact. He had her in there with twelve bulbs of the stuff. He forced them down her throat till she stank like a dog!

They all laugh.

Sasha Father, these are lies.

Lebedev No doubt, but at least they're amusing. More vodka!

Gavrila *pours him another glass.*

Zinaida All I know is that he's broke. If he didn't have Borkin to run the estate for him, then he and his Jewess would have nothing to eat. For us, it's been a real nightmare. For three years he's owed us this terrible debt. Nine thousand roubles!

Babakina (*horrified*) Nine thousand?

Zinaida All thanks to my brilliant husband, of course. Such a great judge of character. It's his choice where we lend. And, believe me, this is not a question of capital. We've not even started to get the interest returned.

Sasha Mother, you have said this over and over.

Zinaida Well . . .

Sasha You talk of nothing else.

Zinaida What business is it of yours?

Sasha How dare you . . . how dare you slander this man when he's done you no harm?

Third Guest If you will allow me, dear Sasha, I respect Ivanov as much as you do. He has welcomed me into his home. But you can hardly deny, through the whole region the man is known as a scoundrel.

Sasha I see.

She looks at him, furious.

And that's your idea of respect?

Third Guest I'm sorry, but there's evidence. We all know. The insurance swindle . . .

Sasha Oh really!

Zinaida It's true!

Third Guest Ivanov bought a herd of cows . . .

Sasha This is nonsense . . .

Zinaida He did!

Third Guest . . . during the cattle epidemic. And then, to make money, he infected them himself.

Sasha The scheme was obviously Borkin's. It has Borkin written all over it. When Ivanov found out, he was furious. All right, you can say he was weak. But he always wants to think well of people. He tries to help them. And how is he thanked? He's been swindled and plundered by every petty crook in the area. People exploit him. He gets exploited because he has a fine heart.

Lebedev Such passion, my God! And in a young girl . . .

Sasha But why? Why do we do this? Why do we talk this rubbish? Ivanov! Ivanov! We talk about nothing else. Do you never ask yourselves why? (*To the young men.*) Oh you lot, you love it. It's easy. So little effort. Let's all talk of one thing! Because of course it would be so much harder for you, you miserable sponges! to think of anything original to say . . .

Lebedev (*laughs*) That's right, you tell them, my dear . . .

Sasha No, that would involve you in actual mental activity. You'd have to try and be witty. You might have to find a new joke. And if you did, you'd risk being attractive to the women. For the moment, thank God, there's no danger of that! But why not? Why not just try it? As a favour? To me? Just once in your life? Think of something brilliant, think of something outrageous, on one single occasion, do something, *do* something even, which would make women sit up? Isn't that what you want? That young women should admire you?

Desire you? Because as things stand, I tell you, you don't have a chance.

Zinaida Well, really!

Sasha *has gone to the door.*

Sasha Until you all change I will never stop saying it: this is a town of dismal young men!

4

Shabyelski *comes in with* **Ivanov** *through the right-hand door.*

Shabyelski Ah the noble sound of oratory! Marvellous! Speech-making, always the perfect birthday activity . . .

He takes **Sasha***'s hand and kisses it.*

May you live a long life, and never have to come back.

Zinaida (*to* **Ivanov**) Nikolai Alekseyevich, what a pleasure to see you!

Lebedev But who's this? Lord God, it's the Count himself!

Shabyelski *reaches his hand towards* **Babakina** *and* **Zinaida**.

Shabyelski Ah, the entire banking community on one sofa! What a treat! (*To* **Zinaida**.) Greetings to you, Zuzu. (*To* **Babakina**.) And to you, my little lemon sherbet.

Zinaida Count, this is such a rare privilege. (*Shouts.*) Gavrila! Do sit down please, everyone.

She goes anxiously to the door but comes back immediately. **Ivanov** *greets everyone silently.* **Sasha** *returns to her place, as* **Lebedev** *embraces and kisses* **Shabyelski**.

Lebedev So where have you popped up from? My God, he's slobbering all over me.

He leads him aside.

Why do we never see you? Are you angry with us or what?

Shabyelski I don't have any horses. What am I meant to do? Come on a bloody broomstick? Nikolai wants me to sit all evening entertaining Anna. Send me your horses, I'll be over like a shot.

Lebedev You're joking. Zinaida'll do anything rather than lend horses. Oh my dear friend, it's such a pleasure to see you. You're all I have left. The only friend I have left from the old days.
'The days we knew of youth and laughter,
Love came first, then grief came after . . .'

He hugs him.

Joking apart, I could almost cry.

Shabyelski Hey, let go of me, you stink like a brewery.

Lebedev I cannot tell you how much I miss my friends. Some days I could slit my wrists with the boredom. (*Quietly.*) Thanks to her banking activities, Zinaida has driven away every decent person we know, and we are left with this lot. Every one a Zulu. A bunch of Wearies and Drearies. That's about it. Have some tea.

Gavrila *has arrived to serve* **Shabyelski**.

Zinaida How many times must I say? With tea you serve jam. Gooseberry jam.

Shabyelski *laughs out loud to* **Ivanov**, *then turns back to* **Lebedev**.

Shabyelski What did I tell you? I had a bet with Nikolai on the way that as soon as we got here the gooseberry jam offensive would begin.

Zinaida Thank you, Count. You still love a joke, I see.

Lebedev She did make twenty barrels of the stuff. What the hell are we to do with it?

Shabyelski *sits by the table.*

Shabyelski Going well, is it? The moneylending? Made a million yet?

Zinaida Oh yes, I know, people think we're rich. But it's all rumour.

Shabyelski Of course. We all know you've no gift for that sort of thing. (*To* **Lebedev**.) Come on, swear on the Bible. Have you reached the million?

Lebedev No use asking me. Ask her.

Shabyelski (*to* **Babakina**) And you must be pretty close to a million as well. Wealth suits you, I must say. Your little pigeon feathers get fluffier by the day.

Babakina Thank you, your Excellency, but I don't care to be mocked like this.

Shabyelski I assure you, madam, there's not a trace of mockery. It's a cry from the heart. I look at you two wealthy women, and I am moved to the bottom of my soul. (*Cheerfully*.) I cannot see either of you without being filled with love.

Zinaida Oh, Count, I see you don't change.

She nods to **Gavrila.**

Gavrila, the candles, please. If they've finished playing, there's no point in wasting the light.

Gavrila *obediently starts blowing out the candles.* **Zinaida** *turns to* **Ivanov**.

Zinaida So tell us, how is your dear wife?

Ivanov Not well, I'm afraid. Today the diagnosis was confirmed. Tuberculosis.

Zinaida What a tragedy. We were just saying. Everyone here loves her so much.

Shabyelski Oh come on, this is crazy! We all know! Tuberculosis is a disease invented by doctors on the perfect pretext for getting close to the female patients. It's a game, for God's sake. Just be grateful in this case her husband doesn't suffer from jealousy.

Ivanov *gestures dismissively*.

Shabyelski Even Anna herself, I don't believe a word she says on the subject. Not a word. It's a good rule. Never trust doctors, lawyers or women. Quackery and lies, that's their stock-in-trade.

Lebedev You really are extraordinary, you know.

Shabyelski Why?

Lebedev It's like misanthropy actually seizes hold of you. Once you start, you talk as if it were lodged in your throat, like a cancer. You speak with the voice of the cancer.

Shabyelski Well, that's charming. What are you suggesting? I'm meant to stay silent?

Lebedev No!

Shabyelski I'm meant to tolerate fools and impostors and liars?

Lebedev Be specific. Which fools? Which impostors?

Shabyelski Well . . .

Lebedev Which liars?

Shabyelski Ah well . . .

Lebedev Well?

Shabyelski *hesitates.*

Shabyelski I don't mean anyone here. Naturally . . .

Lebedev (*simultaneously*) Ah naturally . . .

Shabyelski But present company excepted . . .

Lebedev Oh come on, you know full well, this is all posturing.

Shabyelski You think so? Huh. What do you know? How fortunate you are, my friend, to have no philosophy of life!

Lebedev I will sit here in this room, and one day I will die. *That's* my philosophy (*Shouts.*) Gavrila! Forget philosophy, my friend, we're too old for all that stuff.

Shabyelski I'd say you've Gavrilaed enough already. Your nose looks like a squashed blueberry.

Lebedev *drinks again.*

Lebedev Who cares? It's not as if I'm going anywhere.

Zinaida Why do we never see the doctor? He seems to have forgotten us altogether.

Sasha I can hardly say I missed him. The embodiment of virtue! He can't light a cigarette without sending out the message: 'I'm an honest man.' He's a bore.

Shabyelski I couldn't agree more. What an utter phoney! The scourge of society! 'Make way for the working man!' Squawking like a parrot! And what original views! Any peasant who's making a reasonable living must by definition be doing so at his brothers' expense. And as for the rest of us, if we own more than one jacket, or have a servant to help us get dressed in the morning, then we must all be exploiters. The man is practically exploding with honesty. It's bursting to get out of him. It's like a physical threat. He's aching to punch you in the face with his honesty.

Ivanov I know. He's exhausting. But I like him. He's sincere.

Shabyelski *Sincere*? Oh yes, he's *sincere*. He's throbbing with sincerity. Yesterday, he came up to me. I thought the vein would burst in his neck. I saw it, pulsing away there. 'Count, you repel me,' he said. Oh, thanks very much. I mean, I don't disagree with him. I'm a worthless old fool, I know that. But do I really need to be told? My hair is white. It'll grow white regardless. Do I really need someone to remind me? What sort of honesty is that?

Lebedev Oh come on, you were young once yourself.

Shabyelski Yes, I was young. And I was foolish too. I stood around, like a prig, denouncing the world. But I had a little tact. I never went up to a thief and said 'You're a thief.' There are things you don't do. You don't go into the condemned man's cell and show him the noose. It's not . . . it's not needed. Whereas this man . . . his idea of complete very heaven would be to punch me in the face – not because he wants to, oh God no – but as always in his case, for some blighted principle. He's a man who'd shoot you because he thought it was *right*!

Lebedev That's youth, isn't it?

Shabyelski Not entirely.

Lebedev I had an uncle once, a disciple of Hegel. He used to invite all his friends to the house. Then he'd climb on a chair and denounce them. 'You're the forces of darkness!' he'd say. 'A new life is dawning at last. Blah-di-blah.' He'd lay into them for hours.

Shabyelski And how did they react?

Lebedev How would you react? They carried on drinking. Being denounced? They loved it. They couldn't get enough of it.

5

There is a sudden stir of excitement from outside as **Borkin** *arrives, carrying a parcel, and dressed up to the nines. He is skipping and singing as he arrives, and surrounded by excited young ladies.*

Shabyelski Ah, good news!

Lebedev My goodness me, Borkin is here.

Young Ladies Mikhail Milkhailovich!

Shabyelski It's Borkin. The life and soul of the party.

Borkin Your humble servant, and here in person, my friends.

He goes straight to **Sasha** *and offers her the parcel.*

Bella signora, the universe was honoured the day you were born. As a mark of my own enslavement, may I present you with this small parcel of fireworks of my own manufacture? May they lighten up the night, just as your beauty lightens the gloomy lives we all lead.

He bows theatrically.

Sasha Thank you.

Lebedev (*laughing to* **Ivanov**) Really, you know, you should sack this ridiculous Judas.

Borkin (*to* **Lebedev**) My host! (*To* **Ivanov**.) My patron! (*Sings.*) Nick-a-dick-a-dang-dang, Nick's my man. (*Walking round.*) The rest of you, so many, so beautiful. *Bella* Zinaida! *Bella* Marfusha! *Bella* Avdotya! *Bella, bella, bella*, the whole lot of you! (*Finally.*) And no less a person than the Count.

Shabyelski You see! The party cheers up the moment he arrives.

Borkin Have I missed anyone? I'm exhausted already. So what's going on? What's the news? (*At once to* **Zinaida**.) Just listen, Mumsy, on the way over I couldn't help noticing . . . (*To* **Gavrila**.) Tea, yes, Gavrila, but spare us the gooseberry muck. (*To* **Zinaida**.) Peasants are stripping the bark off your trees. Why don't you rent those trees out?

Lebedev (*to* **Ivanov**) Just sack the little bugger.

Zinaida (*alarmed*) But you're right. It had never even occurred to me.

Borkin *has started doing aerobics.*

Borkin I can't live without exercise. I'm full of energy. Marfusha Babakina, you are looking at a man at the peak of his game. (*Sings.*) 'I see your eyes, and I's your servant, I see your lips and I's your slave . . .'

Zinaida Oh, please, yes, do entertain us. Everyone's so bored.

Borkin Come on, there's no need for these drooping heads, gentlemen. Shall we dance, you luscious yam?

Babakina I can hardly dance tonight. It's the anniversary of my husband's death.

Borkin Then party games, charades, fireworks, what shall it be?

All Fireworks, fireworks.

People begin to follow him out into the garden in a buzz of excitement.

Sasha Why are you so quiet?

Ivanov I've a headache. Your mother said it. We're bored.

Zinaida *turns down the big lamp as she and* **Lebedev** *follow.*

Zinaida If everyone's in the garden, there's no point in wasting candles. Isn't he wonderful? No sooner he's come than we're all feeling more cheerful.

Lebedev I really think we should give them something to eat, my love.

Zinaida Candles everywhere. No wonder people get the idea we're rich.

She is putting more out.

Lebedev My darling, these people are young, they have healthy appetites, they can't survive on nothing . . .

Zinaida The Count never finished his tea. What a waste of sugar.

She goes out.

Lebedev I wish to God you'd just die.

6

Lebedev *follows her out.* **Sasha** *and* **Ivanov** *alone.*

Ivanov It's an extraordinary irony. I used to think and work all the time and I never felt tired. Now I do nothing and I'm completely exhausted. And all because of my conscience. Hour after hour, eating away at me. All the time I feel guilty. But of what? What am I guilty of? I look round, I have no money, my wife is ill, my day goes by in constant, meaningless gossiping and squabbling, I talk gibberish all day with idiots like Borkin. The result is I have come to hate my own home. You are a friend, Sasha, and between friends I hope there is honesty. Is there? I cannot stand the company of a wife who loves me. Tonight I came here purely for distraction, but already I am aching to go home. Forgive me. I'm going. Forgive me.

Sasha Nikolai, I understand you. You are unhappy because you are lonely. Only love . . . love alone can help you.

Ivanov Love? Does love help? Does it? Really? I do mean really. Aren't I a little old? What sort of love? Romance? Oh my God. Hardly. No, it's not romance I need. Anything but. And what goes with it . . . all that unhappiness. God, no! I promise you, I could endure it all, everything I'm experiencing, the poverty, the depression, the loss of my wife, the loneliness, my own useless decay, but the one thing I cannot endure – I *cannot*! – is the contempt I now feel for myself. That above all. I'm half-dead with the shame of it. There are men, I've met them, men who long to be Hamlet, it's all they want, to play the outsider, the superfluous man. To them it's glamorous. Not to me. To me, it's failure. Deep shaming failure. For me – strong, healthy, in my right mind – to be reduced to this state. To me, it's disgrace.

Sasha (*laughing, through tears*) Oh, let's just go, let's run away to America . . .

Ivanov I'm so spent, I couldn't reach that door, let alone America . . .

They head for the garden.

And what about you? What will you do? When I look at this place, when I look at these men you might have to marry, what a fate!

7

Zinaida Savishna *comes from the left-hand door with a pot of jam.*

Ivanov Excuse me, Sasha, I'll be with you in a moment.

Sasha *goes out to the garden.*

Ivanov Zinaida Savishna, forgive me, if I may ask a question?

Zinaida Please. Ask away.

Ivanov Well . . . to be frank, as you may recall, the interest on my loan falls due in what? is it two days? Yes. Two days. It would mean a great deal to me if it could be deferred. As I have no money. In fact.

Zinaida Nikolai Alekseyevich, I am scandalized. Are you out of your mind? I am a respectable woman . . .

Ivanov Of course . . .

Zinaida To make such an obscene suggestion . . .

Ivanov I know.

Zinaida In private.

Ivanov I'm sorry . . .

Zinaida To take advantage. When you've lured me, trapped me alone. To suggest such a thing.

Ivanov I apologize.

Zinaida The deferment of a loan!

Ivanov My fault. My fault. I apologize.

He goes out quickly into the garden.

Zinaida I'm starting to palpitate. My heart!

8

As she goes out by the right-hand door, **Kosykh** *crosses the stage from left to right.*

Kosykh I was holding the ace, the king, the queen, the jack of diamonds, the ace of spaces, and one, just *one* small heart, and she – the ditsy slut – didn't even know to bid a small slam.

9

Kosykh *goes out by the right-hand door.* **Avdotya** *comes in with the* **First Guest** *from the garden.*

Avdotya It's actually some sort of world record. We've been here since five o'clock and we haven't seen so much as a stinking kipper.

First Guest I'd eat the carpet, I'd eat the paintings on the wall . . .

Avdotya What a house! What a way to run a house!

First Guest I'd drop to my knees, like a wolf. I'd savage her. If she came in now, I'd sink my teeth in her thigh . . .

Avdotya Me too. I'd happily rip the flesh from her bones.

First Guest It'd be food! Supper at last! Raw, bloody hunks of our hostess. I'm so hungry I could actually eat a whole leg.

Avdotya There's not even a drink.

First Guest They are always pushing these young women at you. How can you think about women when you haven't even had a drink?

Avdotya Come on, let's go and look . . .

First Guest There's brandy in the dining-room. I know for a fact. Come on, we'll at least get a drink.

10

As they go out by the left-hand door, **Anna** *and* **Lvov** *arrive.*

Anna It's fine. They must all be in the garden. They'll be so glad to see us.

Lvov Why have you brought me to this house of reptiles? This is not a place where honest people should be seen.

Anna Would you mind, Doctor, can I give you a social tip? It's bad manners to take a lady out and keep on about how honest you are. Perhaps it's true but nobody wants to know. I promise you, it's good advice. Don't draw attention to your virtues, let women discover them for themselves. When Nikolai was your age, then he did nothing but sing songs and tell stories. And there wasn't one woman alive who couldn't sense what a fine man he was.

Lvov Please. Don't compare me with Nikolai. I know everything about him.

Anna No. You don't. You're a good man but you know nothing. Let's go into the garden. Nikolai never used to rail against the menagerie. You never heard Nikolai call people reptiles. Or boast about his own superiority. He left people alone to live their own lives. If he spoke at all it was to blame himself for his own impatience, or to express his pity for some poor soul. That's how he was. Forgiving. Not like you . . .

11

As they go out the **First Guest** *and* **Avdotya** *return from the left.*

First Guest Well, if it's not in the dining-room, it must be in the larder. This way.

Avdotya I would happily tear her limb from limb.

12

Babakina *and* **Borkin** *come running in, laughing, from the garden.* **Shabyelski** *comes in, aping the manner of the guests.*

Babakina Oh my God, what a bore! What a bore it all is! A lot of mummies, all stiff as pokers, standing around like a bunch of stuck pigs.

She begins to jump around.

Oh Lord, my bones have all gone rigid. I have to move! I have to live!

Borkin *grabs her by the waist and kisses her on the cheek.* **Shabyelski** *laughs and snaps his fingers.*

Shabyelski Ladies! Gentlemen! Please, some decorum . . .

Babakina Take your hands off me, you brazen seducer, or goodness knows what the Count will think.

Borkin Angel of loveliness, light of my life. (*Kisses her.*) Lend me two thousand three hundred, will you?

Babakina No, absolutely not. No, no no! Do with me what you will. Me, yes. My money, no.

Shabyelski *half-dances around them.*

Shabyelski Look at her, the little pit pony. I have to admit she has her good points . . .

Borkin (*serious*) All right, enough. Now. Let's talk business. Let's level, as they say. Answer me: no prevarication. Yes or no? Which is it?

He points to the **Count**.

On my left, a man in need of a fortune. On my right, a woman in need of a title.

Shabyelski That is putting it a little bit brutally, Misha.

Borkin He needs a minimum of three thousand a year. Tell me, do you want to be a countess or not?

Babakina Please, Misha, this is not . . .

Borkin This is not what?

Babakina This is not the correct way of proceeding. Surely the Count . . . the Count can speak for himself.

Borkin Why?

Babakina I haven't yet discerned the Count's feelings . . .

Borkin His feelings? I don't think his feelings need bother us. His feelings are hardly the point.

Shabyelski *is rubbing his hands and laughing.*

Shabyelski Well, I must say, the odd thing is I find this way of doing things rather erotic. My precious . . . (*Kisses her.*) My sweetheart . . . my little gherkin . . .

Babakina Please, no, this isn't right. Leave me. Go away. No, don't go away. Not yet.

Borkin So come on, tell us, are we in business? Yes or no?

Babakina Could we . . . I mean, I'm just wondering . . . if the Count came to stay with me, say in three days. Then we'd have time. I suppose what I'm asking: is this serious?

Borkin (*angry*) Of course it's serious. What do you think the whole thing's about?

Babakina Oh please, I can't believe it. I feel quite dizzy. A countess! The idea of it. It's impossible. I'm feeling quite ill . . .

13

Borkin *and* **Shabyelski**, *laughing, take* **Babakina** *by the arm, kiss her and lead her through the right-hand door.* **Ivanov** *and* **Sasha** *run in from the garden.* **Ivanov** *is clutching his head in despair.*

Ivanov No, you mustn't. Please. Really, you mustn't. Sasha, I implore you. You have to stop.

Sasha I love you. I love you more than I can tell you. Without you, life has no meaning. To me you are everything on earth.

Ivanov Why? Why me? Please. I understand nothing. Sasha, you mustn't say one word more.

Sasha Since I was a child, it's only been you. I loved you body and soul from the moment I saw you. I love you, Nikolai Alekseyevich. I'll follow you anywhere, to the end of the earth, wherever, to the grave. Only soon, only now, or else I'm going to die.

Ivanov *suddenly laughs.*

Ivanov I can't believe it. To hear those words. To start again. Is there hope again, Sasha? Is there happiness?

He draws her to him.

Oh my sweet youth, my sweet lost youth . . .

Anna *comes in from the garden and stands quite still, watching them.*

Ivanov Yes? We live again. Yes? We start work again. Yes?

They kiss. Then they turn round and both see **Anna**.

Ivanov (*horrified*) Anna!

Act Three

Ivanov'*s study. It is midday. His writing-desk is covered with letters, papers, official envelopes, and odds and ends, including revolvers. On the walls are maps of the area, paintings, shotguns, pistols, sickles and whips. And beside the papers, next to the lamp, is the detritus of a serious drinking session: a carafe of vodka, a plate of herrings, pieces of bread with pickled gherkins.*

1

Shabyelski *and* **Lebedev** *are sitting beside the writing-desk.* **Borkin** *is astride a chair in the middle of the stage.* **Pyotr** *stands by the door.*

Lebedev I like the French. They're good people.

Shabyelski Are they?

Lebedev Of course! French politics are simple. They're not like the Germans. The French at least know what they want. What they want is to rip the Germans' guts out. Who can argue with that?

Shabyelski If only it were true.

Lebedev Get hold of the sausage eaters and de-sausage them.

Shabyelski French, Germans! There's no difference. They're all cowards. You wait! They're like little schoolkids, making rude gestures. Take my word for it. When it comes to it, they're not going to fight.

Borkin He's right. What's the point of fighting anyway? Wasting good money on weapons and guns? You know what I'd do? I'd get hold of that Louis Pasteur. He could round up every dog in the country, inject them with rabies, and send them raging into enemy territory.

Lebedev He's brilliant, eh?

Borkin The Germans'd be foaming at the mouth within days.

Shabyelski The great military strategist!

Lebedev The brain may be small but it's swarming with ideas.

They all laugh. **Lebedev** *turns back to the vodka and pours three glasses.*

There we are. We've fought their war for them, but we haven't had a drink.

Shabyelski Let's have a drink.

Lebedev Good idea. Everyone, good health! Death to the Hun!

They all drink and then eat the zakuski.

No question, the salted herring's the best.

Shabyelski I don't think so. With vodka? No. The gherkin is better. Man struggles up the lonely rockface of evolution, but for all his ingenuity he invents nothing finer than the pickled cucumber. (*To* **Pyotr**.) Pyotr, more gherkins, and some onion pasties to go with them. Hot, mind, hot!

Pyotr *goes.*

Lebedev Caviare's good with vodka. But it's all down to how you prepare it. A quarter of pressed caviare, two lengths of spring onion, a few drops of olive oil and a squeeze of lemon. Mix them together. The smell alone will drive you insane.

Borkin No, for me, the best thing with vodka is gudgeon.

Shabyelski (*contemptuous*) Gudgeon! Gudgeon!

Borkin No, but wait. I'm saying fried. Rolled in breadcrumbs, and fried. So they're dry. Outside, clean and dry. Inside, piping hot and moist. So they crunch between your teeth. Crunch, crunch. Crackle, crackle.

Shabyelski Yesterday at Babakina's she served something good. White mushrooms . . .

Lebedev Ah well yes, white mushrooms . . .

Shabyelski But listen. Steamed with onion and bay leaf and – I don't know – some kind of herbs.

Lebedev Not bad?

Shabyelski When they opened the saucepan, I thought I would faint.

Lebedev Let's drink again.

Shabyelski Very good.

Lebedev One more it is.

All Death to the Hun!

They drink. **Lebedev** *looks at his watch.*

Lebedev So. No Nikolai. I have to go soon. You say you had mushrooms at Babakina's but there's not a whiff of them at my place. Perhaps you might tell us why on earth you're frequenting Babakina's.

Shabyelski *nods at* **Borkin**.

Shabyelski It's his fault. He wants me to marry her.

Lebedev Marry? Uh-huh. How old are you?

Shabyelski Sixty-two.

Lebedev Perfect. The perfect age for it. And the bride – ideal.

Borkin We're not interested in the bride, it's the bride's money we're after.

Lebedev Her money? You're joking. Dream on, Shabyelski.

Borkin All right, you're laughing now but when they're living together, then you'll be sorry.

Shabyelski He's serious, you know. Our great military strategist. He's convinced I'm going to do it.

Borkin Of course you are. What are you saying? Are you getting cold feet?

Shabyelski My dear friend, come on, they've never even been warm.

Borkin You mean, I've been wasting my time?

Shabyelski Oh really! Misha!

Borkin What is this? 'One day I will, next day I won't'? Where does that leave me? Perhaps I might remind you, I gave this woman my word.

Shabyelski Astonishing! The man really does mean it . . .

Borkin (*furious*) How can you think of betraying a perfectly decent and honest woman? Her whole day's spent dreaming of social advancement. She can't eat, she can't sleep. You do have some responsibilities, you know. You can't just walk away.

Shabyelski (*snaps his fingers*) All right, very well. Shall I do it? Out of sheer devilment. Is that what we want? Mark it up as a joke?

2

Lvov *comes in, and at once* **Lebedev** *takes his hand and sings to him.*

Lebedev Ah, the great doctor in person! (*Sings.*) 'I'm scared to death of dying, I'm scared to death of death . . .'

Lvov No sign of Ivanov?

Lebedev No. I've been waiting over an hour.

Lvov *strides impatiently up and down.*

Lebedev So how is Anna today?

Lvov Not good.

Lebedev May I pay my respects?

Lvov I'd rather you didn't. She's sleeping.

Lebedev She's a good person. Truly. The night she fainted at our house, I looked into her face. I saw death written all over it. I don't know what happened. I came in, she was on the floor, Nikolai kneeling beside her, Sasha in tears. For a full week after, Sasha and I couldn't get over it.

Shabyelski (*to* **Lvov**) Yes, now tell me something, Doctor, that I've always wanted to know. Which genius of science was it who first discovered that the closer one puts one's ear to a lady's chest the more fully one may comprehend her sickness? Which branch of medicine takes credit for this discovery? Homeopathy? Allopathy?

Lvov *looks at him with contempt and walks out.*

Shabyelski My God, what a look!

Lebedev Why do you do that? Why do you insult him like that?

Shabyelski Because he's a liar, that's why! He loves it, all that 'Grave situation' and 'I am sorry to have to inform you'. He's lying. I can't stand it.

Lebedev But *why*? Why would he lie?

Shabyelski *gets up and walks around.*

Shabyelski I cannot accept it. That a human being is alive one moment and drops dead the next. It makes no sense. Please, let's change the subject.

3

Kosykh *comes running in, out of breath and quickly shakes everyone's hand.*

Kosykh Hello. Good morning. Is Nikolai home?

Borkin Not yet.

Kosykh In that case, goodbye. I'm so busy. I can't tell you, I'm completely worn out.

He has sat down and got up again. Now he has a vodka and a zakuska.

Lebedev Where've you blown in from?

Kosykh I had a night at Barabonov's. We've only just finished. We were playing the whole night. Right through the night. I lost every penny. Barabonov is useless at cards.

He turns, tearful, to **Borkin** *who moves away at once.*

I'll tell you . . .

Borkin Thanks, but if it's all the same to you . . .

Kosykh I'll describe the situation, so you really understand it: I'm holding hearts and he plays a diamond . . .

Borkin Oh please!

Kosykh I play another heart. He plays another diamond. So, inevitably, I don't have to tell you, I don't have a trick. (*To* **Lebedev**.) All right, so we start playing four clubs. I am holding the ace, the queen, six in all, ten, three of spades . . .

Lebedev (*blocking his ears*) I literally cannot endure this!

Kosykh (*to* **Shabyelski**) No really, it's interesting . . .

Shabyelski Go away, we don't want to know.

Kosykh It's textbook. I have the ace, the queen, six others, and suddenly disaster! No, listen –

Shabyelski *takes a revolver from the desk.*

Shabyelski If you don't shut up, I will shoot.

Kosykh (*waves a hand*) Ah yes, I see, this is how things are going. This is how things are now. Suddenly we are all living in Australia. Live your own life, follow your interest, damn the other man and no common culture at all.

He lifts his hat.

However. I have to go. It's time. Time is precious.

He shakes **Lebedev**'*s hand.*

I pass!

4

They all laugh as **Kosykh** *goes out and bumps into* **Avdotya Nazarovna** *at the door. She lets out a shriek.*

Avdotya Watch where you're going, for goodness' sake.

All Ah, here she is, she's back.

Lebedev The ubiquitous Avdotya Nazarovna.

Avdotya I've found you, my beauties. I've been looking everywhere. Greetings to every one of you.

She shakes all their hands.

Lebedev What are you doing here?

Avdotya Business, sir, business. Matters concerning the Count.

She bows.

The young woman in question sends her regards and tells you that if you do not visit tonight, she will cry her little peepers out. She did ask me to take you aside and whisper this news for your ears only. But as we're all in on this – there are no secrets here – it's not as if we're robbing a bank – this is love, it's out in the open and all above board – so, well . . . I don't usually drink but I must admit on this occasion, perhaps a small one. Just to celebrate.

Lebedev I'll join you.

He pours.

I must say, Avdotya, you're in not bad shape yourself. Given that you seem to have been an old bat for about thirty years now.

Avdotya Thirty? You think? I've lost count. I can't even remember how old I am. I've buried two husbands. I'd be up for the third, but I have no dowry. I've had eight children. No one'll take me without cash.

She takes her glass.

So, here we are, in at the start of something wonderful. May they live to finish what we have begun. Love and happiness to them for the rest of their lives.

She drinks.

Ah now, that is good vodka.

Shabyelski (*laughing, to* **Lebedev**) It's incredible, people do actually think I'm going to do it.

He gets up.

So maybe I will. Why not? Go through with it? Why not?

Lebedev The moment has gone, my friend.

Shabyelski What would you call it? One last crime? One final, glorious act of madness?

Lebedev You long since missed your chance to be rich. The grave, not the wedding bed for us. We've seen the best of our days.

Shabyelski I'm going to do it. Yes, I mean it! As God is my witness, I shall!

5

Ivanov *and* **Lvov** *come in. At once* **Lebedev** *gets up to greet* **Ivanov** *and kiss him.*

Lvov I am only asking for five minutes.

Lebedev Ah, Nikolai! At last, good morning.

Avdotya (*bows*) Ah, good morning, sir.

Lebedev I've been waiting a full hour.

Borkin Do I get a look-in?

Ivanov (*bitterly*) Again! I cannot believe it. Once more you have turned my study into a taproom. I have begged you a thousand times.

He goes to the desk.

KING ALFRED'S COLLEGE
LIBRARY

Look! There's vodka all over my papers. Crumbs. Gherkins. It's disgusting.

Lebedev My fault entirely, dear friend, I apologize. But I have serious things to discuss.

Borkin I was here first.

Lvov I have asked repeatedly.

Ivanov Please, gentlemen, please. I cannot listen to everyone. Pasha comes first.

Lebedev I'm afraid my business is private. I'm sorry, gentlemen.

Shabyelski *and* **Avdotya** *go out.* **Borkin** *follows, and* **Lvov** *last.*

Ivanov I have to ask you, Pasha, drink all you like, that's your problem, but don't infect my uncle. He never used to drink.

Lebedev (*alarmed*) I'm sorry, I didn't know . . .

Ivanov It's bad for him.

Lebedev I'd never noticed . . .

Ivanov Yes and if the drink kills him, it will be me that suffers, not you. What did you want?

There is a pause.

Lebedev Oh Lord, I have to put this carefully, so it doesn't sound callous. You must understand, I'm ashamed before I've even said it. I'm blushing in advance. But please – put yourself in my place. Just imagine the life I lead. What am I? Effectively a serf. Not even a serf. A footcloth, a Negro.

Ivanov Well?

Lebedev I've been dispatched by my wife. Like a parcel. Pay her the interest. Just pay it. I beg you. For the sake of our marriage. I implore you. I can do no other. I'm exhausted. She's bullied me to death.

Ivanov Pasha, I cannot.

Lebedev Please!

Ivanov I have no money at all.

Lebedev I know, I know. But what can I do? She cannot wait. She cannot. If she takes you to court, just imagine. How will Sasha and I ever look you in the eye?

Ivanov I am ashamed as well. I wish the earth would swallow me up. But where can I find money? Where? My only hope is the harvest.

Lebedev (*shouts*) She can't wait!

There is a pause.

Ivanov Yes, your situation is tricky but mine is far worse. I've racked my brains, but there's nothing.

Lebedev Go to Milkbakh. He owes you sixteen thousand.

Ivanov Oh . . .

He makes a gesture of despair.

Lebedev Look, I know you won't like this, but just humour an old drunkard for once. Here we are. Both graduates of Moscow University. Both students. Both liberals. With ideas and values in common. And, what's more, friends, I would hope.

He takes money from his wallet and puts it on the table.

This is money I've stashed away for myself. It can't be traced. Eleven hundred. Think of it as a loan. Yes? Swallow your pride. I promise you, if our positions were reversed, I would take what you gave me, and without a second thought.

There is a pause.

There it is. Go over to the house, put it in her hand and say to her, 'Zinaida Savishna, here is your money, drop dead.' But for God's sake don't tell her where you got it, or she'll choke me to death with gooseberry jam.

He looks **Ivanov** *in the face. Then he takes back the money and quickly puts it in his pocket.*

I'm sorry, a joke. I meant it as a joke. A joke in bad taste. Forgive me.

There is a pause.

Have you lost hope altogether?

Ivanov *gestures again.*

Lebedev I understand. It's . . . existence. The nature of it, I mean. Calm times, then troubled. Man? I'd say almost like a samovar. That's right. He cannot sit cold on the shelf for ever. The moment will come when the burning charcoal arrives. All right, it's a rotten analogy, but it's the best I can do. (*Sighs.*) Bad times are good for you. If you see what I mean. That's why I'm not worried for you. Though I am disturbed when . . . when I hear people talking. Why are there so many rumours? Why are they all about you, Nikolai? What started it? One day you're a murderer, the next day you're a thief, the next the police are coming to arrest you . . .

Ivanov It means nothing. My head hurts.

Lebedev Try not thinking.

Ivanov I don't think.

Lebedev Oh, let it all go to hell. Why not? Why don't you visit us any more? Sasha's fond of you. She understands you. She's a decent person. She's loyal and sincere. I can't think where she gets it from. Certainly not her mother, still less from me. There must have been some sort of illicit union I never heard about. I look at her and can't believe that this drunk with a luminous nose could have such a jewel for a daughter. Why don't you come over, do all your brilliant talking together? Really. Sasha'll cheer you up.

There is a pause.

Ivanov My friend, please leave me alone.

Lebedev All right, I understand. Truly.

He looks quickly, then kisses **Ivanov**.

I understand. Farewell. New school, opening today. Have to be there.

He moves to the door, then stops.

I've always said my daughter was clever. Yesterday we were discussing all these rumours about you and she said 'Papa, glow-worms shine at night to make it easier for birds to see them and eat them. So good people only exist so that gossip and rumour may have somewhere to feed.' Not bad, eh? I told you. A genius. Watch out, George Sand.

Ivanov Pasha!

He stops him.

What is wrong with me?

Lebedev Ah, yes. Good question. I've not wanted to ask. I thought perhaps your troubles had got the better of you. But you're not the type. Usually you overcome misfortune. So, well . . . it's something else. But I don't know what.

Ivanov Me neither. Though sometimes . . . oh Lord, no. No it's not that.

There is a pause.

The nearest I can get: I used to have a workman. Semion, he was called, you remember? At harvest-time he wanted to show off in front of the girls, so he loaded two sacks of rye at once. He strained his back. And he died soon after. That's how I feel. As if my back has been broken. School, university, agriculture, village education, civic projects . . . From the start I was set on doing everything differently. I married differently, I lived differently, took more risks, used my own money, threw it away. I was happier and unhappier than anyone else in the region. But these things were like sacks. I loaded them on my back. And now it's snapped, it's literally given way. At twenty we're all heroes, we can do anything, can't we? By thirty, we're already exhausted. How do you . . . I ask, how you explain it? We're so tired. It's as if . . . I don't know . . . what can I say to you? Go, Pasha, go. Leave me. You must be so tired of me.

Lebedev You know what it is?

He gestures round.

This place. These surroundings. They are what's killing you.

Ivanov (*smiles*) No. That's the usual excuse. It's stupid.

Lebedev Yes. Well, no doubt yes you're right, it's stupid. I said it. And it's stupid. I'll get out of your way.

6

Lebedev *leaves.* **Ivanov** *is alone.*

Ivanov How spent I am, how I despise myself. It's only a drunk like Pasha who can still respect me. I hear my own voice and I hate it. I look at my own hands, my clothes, my feet even and I seem to know them too well. Just a year ago! That's what's so crazy, I was healthy and strong. I was cheerful, I worked. I could make sentences. When I talked, strong men wept and even idiots were inspired. When I saw unhappiness, I cried. When I saw evil, I raged. The inspiration was there. I sat every night at my desk, I felt the poetry of the evening, from the sun's going down to the sun's rising. I worked through the night in the quiet and I dreamed. I looked into the future like a child looking into its mother's eyes. But now . . . I search for faith, I spend days and nights in idleness, in doing-nothingness, my mind, my body in permanent revolt. I look out of the window: my estate is in ruins and my forests are under the axe.

He weeps.

It needs me. The land needs me. And I have no hope, no expectation. My sense of tomorrow is gone. I swore to love Anna for ever. Eternal love, that's what I promised. I opened her eyes, I offered her a future of which she'd never even dreamed. Yet these last five years I've watched her fading, growing weaker every day, sapped by the struggle, but never once turning to me, never uttering a single word of reproach. And how have I rewarded her? By ceasing to love her. Why? To what end? Somebody explain! My own wife is dying, her days are numbered and all I can do is run from her awful pleading eyes, from her face, from her cough. The shame, the shame of it . . .

There is a pause.

And this child, Sasha, touched by my unhappiness. She declares her love to this ludicrous old man, and he is charmed, as if by music. He shudders back into life and stands there, shaking, spellbound, crying out 'A new life! Happiness!' Then wakes the next day, like a cheap drunk in a brothel. What is it? Why am I heading for the cliff? Why am I drawn to it? What's happened to my strength? A gun goes off, a servant drops a dish, my wife says the wrong thing, and suddenly . . .

There is a pause.

Do it. Do it, Nikolai. Put a bullet in your brain. I don't understand.

Lvov *comes in.*

Lvov Nikolai Alekseyevich, it is essential we talk.

Ivanov We talk every day, Doctor, there must be some sort of human limit.

Lvov Will you just let me speak?

Ivanov You speak every day, sometimes three times a day, and I still have no idea what you want from me.

Lvov I speak plainly and to the point. Only a man without a heart could misunderstand me.

Ivanov Usually you make three points. One, my wife is dying. Two, it's my fault. Three, you are an honest man. So, tell me, in which order do you wish to put these points today?

Lvov I need to speak out because I cannot endure cruelty. It is the cruelty of things that dismays me. In the next room, a woman is dying. The least she deserves is to see her own parents. They know full well that she loves them, that she needs to see them, but because of their pride – the stubbornness of their religion – they refuse to relent. Still they condemn her! And you are the man for whom she sacrificed everything, even her own family. Yet without apology and with no sense of shame you go tripping over to Lebedev's, for purposes which are clear to us all.

Ivanov You're wrong. I haven't been there for weeks.

Lvov (*not listening*) People tell me I'm young, but I have learnt one thing in life. One must be straight with people. One must be blunt. I have watched you, Ivanov. I have seen you. And I have seen through you. You are longing for her death. Yes, I know what I'm saying. You will welcome her death because it will give you the chance to move on. But I have come today in the name of humanity to ask you to wait. If nothing else, just wait. Give Anna her time, let her die in the goodness of time. Don't drive this woman to the grave. Is there really such a rush? Would you lose this new girl if you slowed down? You are so accomplished, so proficient, so adept . . . surely the seduction of any woman will not detain you for long. Why do you need your present wife to die straight away?

Ivanov Doctor! What sort of doctor are you?

Lvov Oh please! Who are you trying to fool?

Ivanov How little you understand if you expect me to control myself while you say these things to me.

Lvov Ivanov, the mask is off! It's been off for months. Your whole life is a fake.

Ivanov You're such a clever man, Doctor. A clever doctor. For you, things are easy. They are what they seem to be. I married Anna to get her fortune. I didn't get it. I made a mistake, so now I'm trying to dispose of her, so I can fix on somebody else and get their money instead. Yes? Isn't that what you think? How simple human beings are to you. What uncomplicated machines! Well no, actually, Doctor. Look a little closer. There are so many cogs in us, so many wheels, so many valves that we judge each other at our own peril. I don't understand you. You don't understand me. And least of all do we understand ourselves. Least of all. You may be a great doctor, but about humanity you know nothing. Don't be so damnably self-confident. Listen and learn.

Lvov What a convenient philosophy! No such words as 'good' or 'bad'? No 'right', no 'wrong'. Everything 'complicated'. 'Complex'. Is that right?

Ivanov Look. You come to see me all the time. Not a day goes by. Plainly it's not for a meeting of minds. So then why? You're obsessed with me. Have you ever looked inside yourself? Have you ever asked yourself why? Examined your own behaviour? Asked what you want from me?

He is suddenly furious.

Just who am I speaking to? My wife's doctor or the counsel for the prosecution?

Lvov I'm a doctor. It's a clinical judgement. I am instructing you: change your ways, you are killing your wife.

Ivanov Ways? My ways? Please, you understand me better than I do myself. Tell me what changing my ways would entail.

Lvov You know full well.

Ivanov No. Tell me. How would you wish me to change?

Lvov I would wish you . . . to be more discreet.

Ivanov Oh my God, out! Out of here!

He drinks some water.

How dare you? How *dare* you? Yes, I shall answer to God, I know that, for everything I am, for everything I have done. But I do not have to answer to you. You have no right to torment me.

Lvov I? You say I torment *you*? Do you have any idea? Do you have any idea of what you have done to me? Before I came to this godforsaken region, I believed in humanity. I knew people were stupid. I made allowances. But never once did I dream that people could be criminal, that they could be deliberately evil. I loved people. I respected them. I had faith. Until I met you.

Ivanov I've heard this before.

Lvov And that makes it not true?

He looks and sees **Sasha** *come in, wearing a riding dress.*

Ah. Well then. My point is made for me. At least now things are clear.

7

Lvov *shrugs his shoulders and goes out.* **Ivanov** *is taken aback by* **Sasha**'*s appearance.*

Ivanov Sasha . . .

Sasha Yes. What's wrong?

Ivanov What are you doing here? Why have you come?

Sasha You never visit, you no longer visit us . . .

Ivanov For goodness' sake, this is madness. Didn't you think? Did you never consider the effect on my wife?

Sasha I thought of it. I came round the back.

Ivanov Sasha, I cannot believe it. My wife is already in torment. She's at death's door. And you choose to come here . . .

Sasha What else could I do? You don't answer my letters. All day I think about you. I imagine you suffering. I've not slept. Not one single night.

She looks at him a moment.

All right, I'll go. Just tell me: are you all right?

Ivanov All right? How can I be all right? I'm completely exhausted. The whole world is beating a path to my door. Now you! I'm almost insane with guilt.

Sasha Ah yes, guilt . . .

Ivanov Yes!

Sasha Guilt! How you love it. What's your crime, then? Name it. Go on.

Ivanov *says nothing.*

Sasha Sinners surely can name their own sin. What's yours? Forgery?

Ivanov (*turning away*) Sasha . . .

Sasha What have you been doing? Printing up banknotes?

Ivanov That isn't funny!

Sasha Isn't it? You feel guilty because you've stopped loving a woman. Isn't that right?

Ivanov I don't know. I don't know!

Sasha So why is that a sin? Are you not allowed feelings? It was hardly at your wish. Or is the sin that she happened to walk into a room? Again, it's hardly . . .

Ivanov I know. And so on. These words we all use! 'Allowed our own feelings'! 'It isn't at my wish.' These tawdry, exhausted little phrases that human beings love to fool themselves with.

Sasha Whatever I say, you tear it apart.

She looks at a painting.

This dog is good, isn't it? Was this done from life?

Ivanov Yes, from life. And this so-called romance we are having, also a cliché. It's out of a book. 'He had lost his way, he had stumbled. Then she reached out a hand to save him.' That's how it happens in novels.

Sasha It also happens in life.

Ivanov Life! Goodness, life . . .

Sasha Yes!

Ivanov Which you understand so instinctively. Oh and how you relish it when I'm unhappy!

Sasha Do I?

Ivanov Yes. The unhappier the better! Because it means you're in love with Hamlet. But to me, you see, Hamlet's an idiot. He's a figure of fun. Healthy people laugh at their own weaknesses. They mock self-indulgence. But naturally that holds no appeal for you. Insufficiently romantic! No, you're only happy in the ambulance corps. Here come the nurses! All in freshly starched linen, riding in like the cavalry to bandage the wounds! Oh Lord, I'm sorry. Something must break today . . . the truth is, I'm longing for violence . . .

Sasha Good. Let it out. You're angry. Smash some china. Why not? You're entitled. After all, it's my fault. I've done something stupid. I should never have come. So yell at me. Please.

There is a pause.

Well?

Ivanov It's funny.

Sasha Good then, it's funny. It's *something*, thank goodness. Anything. Just as long as you manage to smile once again.

Ivanov (*laughs*) I look at you when you're doing your cavalry acting. There's this wonderful look on your face. Pure innocence. As if you were watching a comet. Your pupils get bigger. Wait, there's some dust on your coat.

He brushes some dirt off her shoulder.

Why is it attractive for a woman to be innocent when it's so ridiculous in a man? Why are you all drawn to despair?

Sasha Are we?

Ivanov When a man is strong and happy you ignore him completely, but the moment he slides downhill, whoosh, you're off after him like a shot.

He presses his face to her shoulder.

Let me rest and forget, if only for a moment.

There is a silence, the two of them still.

Sasha There's so much you don't understand. For men, love is just how-are-you-darling? It's just a stroll in the garden. One day, it'll be a few tears at the graveside. But for us? No, it has to be life itself. If you climb a mountain, I'll climb with you. Jump over the cliff: I'll jump. I never told you, there was a day about three years ago when you came to our door, sunburned, tired, covered in dust. You were fresh from harvesting. You asked for a drink. When I brought you the glass, you were laid out on the sofa, dead to the world. You slept in our house and I stood at the door, guarding you, keeping people away. I stood for a full twelve hours. I've never been happier in my life. The more effort you have to make, the better love is.

Pyotr *appears silently with a plate of hot pasties.*

Pyotr Pasties.

Ivanov What? What did you say?

Pyotr Hot pasties. The Count ordered them.

Ivanov Go away.

Pyotr *turns and goes out.* **Ivanov** *shrugs, suddenly cheerful.*

Ivanov My dear girl, how wonderful you are. And how stupid I've been, playing at tragedy. Boo-hoo. Upsetting people wherever I go.

He laughs and moves quickly away.

You have to go, Sasha. We're forgetting ourselves.

Sasha I know. I'm off. I fear the honest doctor may feel it's his duty to tell Anna Petrovna I was here. So, please, go to her and stay by her bed. Sit. If you need to, sit for a year. If you need to stay ten years, stay ten. But do your duty. Grieve with her and ask her forgiveness. Weep. It's right. And above all don't neglect your estate.

Ivanov Oh God, I'm under Matron's orders again.

Sasha God bless you, Nikolai. You may now put me out of your mind altogether. It's fine. As long as you write me a letter. Say, in two weeks. I'd be grateful. And I shall write to you.

8

Borkin *looks in the door and then sees* **Sasha**.

Borkin Nikolai, is it my turn? Oh Good Lord, I'm sorry, I didn't see you there. *Bonjour, mam'selle.*

He bows. **Sasha** *is embarrassed.*

Sasha How do you do?

Borkin My goodness, look at you! Prettier than ever, and if I may say so, you've filled out.

Sasha (*to* **Ivanov**) So, I must go, Nikolai Alekseyevich. I must go.

She goes out.

Borkin What a vision! Extraordinary! I came for prose and stumbled across poetry (*Sings.*) 'A bird in flight, a streak of light . . .'

Ivanov *walks up and down, upset.* **Borkin** *sits down.*

Borkin She really does have something, doesn't she? Something none of the others have. She's almost like a fantasy. Financially, she's actually the best prospect in the district, but her mother's such a skunk nobody wants to go near the daughter. Who can blame them? I mean, Sasha'll get the lot when her mother dies, but until then she's only getting ten thousand and the odd toffee apple, and even for *that* she's expected to say thank you all day.

He searches through his pockets and finds his cigar-case.

Cigars. Fancy one? They're not bad. They're quite smokeable.

Ivanov *approaches* **Borkin** *furious.*

Ivanov Get out! Get out of this house for ever!

Borkin *half-rises, dropping his cigar.*

Ivanov Now! This very minute!

Borkin Hold on. What is this? What have I done?

Ivanov Where did you get those cigars? Do you think I don't know?

Borkin Cigars? Is this about the cigars?

Ivanov And where you take that old man every day, and what you're up to with him?

Borkin What's that got to do with you?

Ivanov Everyone in the district knows what you're doing. You're low. You're dishonest. You bring disgrace on this household. We have nothing in common, and I insist you leave my house this instant.

Borkin Oi-oi-oy! *Quel mauvais humeur*! Well, I refuse to rise to it. Please, insult me as much as you like.

He picks up his cigar.

As for these depressions of yours, can I just say they're a thundering bore? You're not an adolescent any more.

Ivanov Did you not hear me? You think you can play with me?

9

Ivanov *is now shaking with rage.* **Anna Petrovna** *comes in.*

Borkin Ah well, if Anna Petrovna is here . . . then fine. That's different.

Borkin *goes out.* **Ivanov** *stops by the desk and stands, his head bowed.*

Anna What was she doing here?

A pause.

I need to know. Why did she come here?

Ivanov Don't ask.

Anna What was she doing here?

Ivanov I am profoundly guilty. Punish me any way you choose. But please, don't ask any more. I've no strength to tell you.

Anna Now I see. Now I begin to see you. At last I see the kind of person you are. A man without honour.

Ivanov No!

Anna You came to me, and lied. I gave up my religion, my family. I even gave up my name. You talked to me about goodness and truth. You told me you loved me. But the words were dirt. And I believed every word.

Ivanov Anna, I have never lied to you.

Anna I have lived here with you five years, I've suffered and grown ill, but I did not stop loving you for one moment. You were my god. And all that time you have been deceiving me . . .

Ivanov Anna, accuse me of anything but not of dishonesty. I have never once lied in my life. Accuse me of anything, but not of dishonesty.

Anna Everything now makes sense to me. You married me because you thought my parents would give in . . .

Ivanov No!

Anna You thought I'd inherit.

Ivanov Oh my God, Anna, no, please don't torment me . . .

Ivanov *cries.*

Anna Be quiet! And now you've a fresh plan. Now everything is clear to me. I understand everything.

She cries.

You have never loved me. You have never been faithful. Never.

Ivanov Anna, these are lies. Say what you feel, but don't degrade me with lies.

Anna Crooked and dishonest! You owe money to Lebedev, so now you are going to seduce his daughter. You want to trick her just as you tricked me. It's the truth.

Ivanov (*gasping*) Please, Anna, be quiet.

Anna I will not be quiet!

Ivanov I beg you, say nothing else. The anger is killing me. I am going to insult you.

Anna All the time you've pleaded innocence. You've manipulated us all. You've put schemes in Borkin's head, then blamed them on him . . .

Ivanov Be silent. I beg you, be silent. I cannot stop myself. The words will burst out of me.

He shouts.

You dirty Jew.

Anna I will never be quiet. Never again. Not after what you've said to me, not after what you've done . . .

Ivanov You refuse? You refuse to be silent?

He struggles with himself.

In the name of God . . .

Anna Now go off and start swindling Lebedev.

Ivanov You are going to die. I have spoken to the doctor. You are going to die very soon.

Anna *sits down. Her voice fades.*

Anna When did he say that?

There is a pause. **Ivanov** *clutches his head with his hands.*

Ivanov Oh my God, the evil! How evil I am!

Act Four

A full year has passed. One of the drawing-rooms in the Lebedevs' house. At the front is an arch, dividing it from the ballroom. There are doors left and right. There are old bronzes and family portraits. There are decorations for a party. There is a piano, with violin and cello nearby. Throughout the act visitors pass to and fro through the ballroom, all in evening-dress.

1

Lvov *comes in and looks at his watch.*

Lvov Past four already. Soon the blessing, and in no time at all, the wedding itself. So there we are. The triumph for the forces of good! His first wife dead, and now another lined up, waiting to be fleeced. Turn her upside down, shake her pockets out, and then throw her in the same grave as Anna. Put her in a ditch with the last one. All while pretending you're a man of integrity.

There is a pause.

He thinks he's in seventh heaven and will live to a ripe old age and die with a clear conscience. No! I'm here to tell him he won't. I shall wrench the mask from the hypocrite. I shall seize him in his hiding-place, and throw him burning into the deepest pit in hell! Citizens have duties. It's the duty of the honest man. But by what means? Talk to Lebedev? Hardly. A waste of breath. Start a row? Create a scandal? Provoke a duel? Oh, God, I'm nervous now. My stomach. I'm not thinking clearly. Think clearly. What's best? A duel?

2

Kosykh *comes in and at once addresses* **Lvov** *cheerfully.*

Kosykh Ah, so listen, this is interesting: yesterday I bid a small slam in clubs and won a big one instead. I was playing with Barabonov . . .

Lvov I'm sorry, I'm afraid I don't play cards myself, so I can't share your enthusiasm. Has the blessing happened?

Kosykh Not yet. They're trying to calm Zinaida down. She's screaming like a fishwife. Can't face losing the dowry.

Lvov What about losing her daughter?

Kosykh No, not the daughter, the dowry. What's more, it means writing off a debt. Not even she can sue her own son-in-law.

3

Babakina *walks by, dressed to the nines, and* **Kosykh** *at once starts giggling behind her back. But she catches him.*

Babakina Philistine!

Kosykh *touches her waist with his finger and laughs loudly.*

Babakina Peasant!

She goes out. **Kosykh** *goes on laughing.*

Kosykh The woman's gone mad. She was all right until she started dreaming of elevation. Now you can't go near her.

He imitates her.

'Peasant!'

Lvov Kosykh, I have a question to ask you. Tell me honestly. What do you think of Ivanov?

Kosykh Truthfully?

Lvov Yes.

Kosykh Very little. He bids trumps almost regardless of what's in his hand.

Lvov No, I mean, is he a good man?

Kosykh A good man? Ivanov? What do you think? He's a strategist. Surely you can see that. He and the Count are two of a kind. It's all a game. Ivanov is a consummate games-player. That's what he is. He lost out to the Jewess, so now it's double or quits. He'll take Zinaida's money, the Count'll take Babakina's. And the two women'll be out on the street within a year. That's the way of it, that's the game. You watch, I'm expecting a perfectly played hand. Doctor, you're looking pale. Are you all right?

Lvov I'm fine. Perhaps I've been drinking too much.

4

Lebedev *comes in with* **Sasha**, *sending* **Lvov** *and* **Kosykh** *away.*

Lebedev We can talk in here. You two hooligans, join the ladies, please. I need privacy.

Kosykh *snaps his fingers as he passes* **Sasha**.

Kosykh Natty as the queen of trumps, and just as welcome.

Lebedev Come on, caveman, out!

Kosykh *and* **Lvov** *go.*

Lebedev Sit down, Sasha, that's right.

He sits himself.

Now. I want you to listen in the appropriate manner. With the appropriate deference. All right? I'm here at your mother's bidding. You understand? Although I shall be speaking, it will only be as her representative. Her mouthpiece.

Sasha For goodness' sake, Papa, get on with it.

Lebedev Your dowry. Will be fifteen thousand roubles in silver. Hold on, let me finish. There's more to come. The round figure, the official figure is fifteen. However. Since Nikolai Alekseyevich happens to owe your mother nine thousand, she has decided that the figure which will actually be surrendered, will be nearer . . . well . . . as you might say . . . six.

Sasha Why are you telling me this?

Lebedev Because your mother has asked me to.

Sasha For what possible purpose? If you had the slightest respect for me, you wouldn't dream of telling me. I don't want your dowry . . .

Lebedev Oh now, Sasha, please . . .

Sasha I didn't ask for it and I certainly have no intention of taking it.

Lebedev Why take it out on me? You're meant to listen, you are at least meant to *listen* to the offer. It's only good manners. Give it a sniff. But you're so desperate to appear progressive, you can't even wait two minutes to turn it down.

Sasha I find this kind of talk about money demeaning.

Lebedev Demeaning! Oh please. I'm the intermediary, that's all. On one side I have a wife who thinks of nothing else, all day she sits there counting her kopeks as if her life depended on it, and on the other, here before me – the spirit of emancipation! Despises her own father for even daring to mention the subject. Well, forgive me! I'm just the poor idiot who gets mashed between the two of you.

He goes to the door.

Do you not see? Can you not even tell? I hate this. I hate it.

Sasha What do you hate?

Lebedev I hate the whole thing.

Sasha What whole thing?

Lebedev Do you really want me to say? Should I spoil your wedding day? When you marry, I shall not be able to look?

He goes up to **Sasha**, *suddenly tender.*

Forgive me, Sasha, maybe there is something here, something in this marriage which is passing me by. Since you're involved, then I've no doubt it's something pure, something noble, something high-minded. But to this bulbous old nose, it smells wrong. How do I say this to you? Look at you. You're beautiful, you're young. And he? An exhausted widower who has already worn himself out. Worse, a man whom nobody understands.

He kisses her.

Sasha, I'm sorry. There is something not wholesome. People are talking, but with good reason. I'll say it one time only. His wife dies and at once he marries you.

He changes his tone to briskness at once.

Now. I sound like an old woman. Forgive me. I'm becoming absurd. I'm like some ghastly old maid. Take no notice. Follow your own heart.

Sasha My heart?

Lebedev Yes.

There is a pause.

Sasha Then tell me. Tell me it's right. Help me. In my own heart . . . I don't know. It's unbearable. If you had any idea of what I've been through. Cheer me up, Papa. Cheer me up, my darling, tell me what to do.

Lebedev What to do?

Sasha I'm frightened to death.

She looks round.

Sometimes I think I don't understand him and I am terrified I never will. All the time we've been engaged he hasn't smiled once. Nor once looked me in the eye. All I hear is endless complaint, guilt, hints, rambling allusions. Talk of unnamed crimes. He shakes. Physically. There are times when it seems to me I don't love him as I should. As I need to. When he comes here, he begins to talk, and I feel . . . impatient. What does that say? Tell me, Papa, tell me what that says.

Lebedev My dear child, my dear sweet child, I beg you, let him go.

Sasha (*terrified*) What do you mean?

Lebedev Just do it.

Sasha Let him go?

Lebedev Why not?

Sasha How can I? I can't!

Lebedev We'll ride through it. A year's scandal, my God, two years maybe . . .

Sasha How can I?

Lebedev . . . but better that, better ride out the gossip than ruin your whole life.

Sasha No. You mustn't say that. We have to fight, Father, it's our duty. We have a duty to fight. It's true. This is a fine upstanding man and my job in life is to understand him. That's my calling. I'll set him on his feet and he'll start again.

Lebedev That's not a calling, that's a prison sentence.

Sasha Father, I have to ask you: today I said things to you I would say to no one else. Now you must forget them. Tell no one.

Lebedev What's happening? Has the whole world got too clever for me? Or has it just got too stupid?

5

Shabyelski *appears.*

Shabyelski Oh damn and blast everyone. Myself included. Me most of all. May we all go to hell!

Lebedev What's going on?

Shabyelski I am preparing myself, my dear friend, to do something contemptible, for which everyone will despise me. And rightly. I am going through with it. I've instructed Borkin to announce my engagement. Yes! Today.

He laughs.

The world is a whorehouse, I shall simply be one more whore.

Lebedev Oh come on, pull yourself together, man. Whorehouse? Madhouse!

Shabyelski What difference does it make? Take me to either. Take me to both. Take me to both at once! How can it be worse than living among these trivial, tenth-rate, talentless people? I'm glutted with self-disgust. I hear myself speak and don't even believe my own words.

Lebedev There's meant to be a wedding. Shall I tell you what's best? Stuff an oily rag in your mouth and set light to it. Go breathe fire over everyone. Better still, go home. We're meant to be cheerful, and here you are, squawking like a demented raven. I mean it.

Shabyelski *leans over the piano and starts to cry.*

Lebedev Oh Lord, look, I'm sorry. My dear friend! Matyusha, have I offended you? Please! Forgive an old drunkard. Have a glass of water.

Shabyelski I don't want it.

He lifts his head.

Lebedev Why are you crying?

Shabyelski I shouldn't say.

Lebedev Come on, my dear fellow, tell me. What's the reason?

Shabyelski Just for a moment, I looked across at the cello over there. I remembered the little Jew, I remembered Anna.

Lebedev What great timing! My God. All respect to her, may she rest in peace, but this is hardly the moment.

Shabyelski We played duets. She was remarkable. Truly. A truly remarkable woman.

Sasha *starts to cry as well.*

Lebedev Oh Lord, now it's both of them. Can we just . . . does anyone mind if we don't actually cry in sight of the guests?

Shabyelski Pasha, we can all be happy, as long as we have hope. But I am a man without hope.

Lebedev I do see that, my friend. Believe me, I see it. No children, no money, no future. I understand. But what can I do?

He turns to **Sasha**.

What started you off?

Shabyelski Pasha, just give me some money. Give me some. I'll pay you back. Not in this world, admittedly. But in the next. I'll go to Paris and sit by my wife's grave. I've been generous, you know that, in my lifetime I have given away half my fortune. I have the right to ask. I'm asking a friend. Please.

Lebedev Look . . . actual money. I don't have any. Not of my own. But all right . . . if I can, I will. It's not a promise but . . . I will find you some. (*Aside*.) They get to you. Eventually they wear you down.

6

Babakina *comes in and heads for* **Shabyelski** *whom she hits on the arm with her fan.*

Babakina Now well really! Where's my handsome hero? How can you have left me by myself?

Shabyelski (*with loathing*) All too easily.

Babakina What?

Shabyelski Go away. I hate you.

Babakina What are you saying?

Shabyelski What I have long dreamed of saying. Leave me, leave me alone for ever!

Babakina Leave you?

Shabyelski Yes. My pom-pom, my pigeon, my ootsy-tootsy little toffee apple . . .

Babakina How dare you? Is it all money? Is it all just money for you?

Shabyelski No. Taste comes into it as well.

Babakina Very well. I will spite you all. I will take a vow. I will never marry again.

Zinaida *appears in a new dress, crying.*

Zinaida Someone's coming. It must be the best man . . .

Lebedev Oh for God's sake . . .

Sasha (*imploring*) Oh Mother . . .

Zinaida It must be time for the blessing already.

Lebedev Ah, wonderful! Now we have a full house. A full quartet! This is marvellous. We shall all be washed away.

He starts to cry, as **Sasha** *takes her mother in her arms.*

Oh God!

Zinaida If he had one ounce . . . one *ounce* of self-respect he would have paid his debt before proposing.

7

Ivanov *comes in, wearing a tail-coat and gloves.*

Lebedev Now this is the limit! What on earth is this?

Sasha Nikolai, why are you here?

Ivanov I am sorry, ladies and gentlemen, but I must speak with Sasha alone.

Lebedev It's impossible. It can't be done, for the groom to speak to the bride. You should meet in the church.

Ivanov Pasha, I'm sorry. I have no choice.

8

Lebedev *shrugs his shoulders, then he,* **Zinaida**, **Babakina** *and* **Shabyelski** *all go out.* **Sasha** *is defiant when they are left alone.*

Sasha What do you want from me?

Ivanov Sasha, as I dressed for my wedding, I looked in the mirror. And as I looked, I saw grey hair. This must now be the end of it. I feel this rage. Your whole life stretches before you . . .

Sasha I know. You've told me. You've told me repeatedly. Get over to the church, and don't hold people up.

Ivanov I'm not going to the church. I'm going back to my house. You must take your family to one side and simply inform them: the wedding is off. We've been acting. I've been playing Hamlet and you've been playing the missionary. Shall I tell you? Both of us have exhausted our roles.

Sasha (*exploding*) What is this? How dare you? I simply won't listen.

Ivanov Perhaps you won't listen, but I shall still talk.

Sasha What are you doing here? It's a joke.

Ivanov A joke? Well, that would be welcome. I'd love that.

Sasha This is our wedding day!

Ivanov A joke is exactly what I'd most like it to be. Let the whole world laugh at me, please!

He laughs.

Do you know what it feels like? To watch yourself wither? To know you have gone on living too long? To look up at the sun and see it still shining? It shines regardless. To look at an ant, carrying its burden. Even an ant can be happy with its lot. To look round, to see people's faces – this person thinks I'm a phoney. Another one pities me. Another one thinks I need help! And worst of all, to catch people listening respectfully, as if by listening they could actually learn! People think there's something deep about despair. But there isn't. As if I could found a new religion, and impart some earth-shattering truth. I still have some pride. As I came here, laughing at my own absurdity, it seemed to me the birds and the trees were beginning to laugh at me too.

Sasha This isn't rage. This is madness.

Ivanov Madness? This is cold sanity. Yes, the rage is speaking. But the rage tells the truth. You and I . . . we're in love, but we cannot marry. I have a perfect right to destroy my own life, but I have no right to destroy other people's. Yes. And that's what I did to my first wife. By my endless complaining. And now it's the same with you. Since we met, you've stopped laughing. You've aged. You look five years older. Your father who once was at peace with the world now stands round in confusion. Lost. The only thing I have ever wanted: to try to be honest! To try to tell the truth. And the effect has been to spread dissatisfaction around me wherever I go. I spread contagion. Everywhere I spread my contempt. As if I was doing life a favour by consenting to be alive! Oh, let me be damned in hell.

Sasha Do you not see? This is the moment I've longed for.

Ivanov Why?

Sasha This is the step you're now ready to take. At last, here, today, before this wedding, you see your condition clearly. You see it and you resolve to start a new life.

Ivanov A new life?

Sasha Yes.

Ivanov How? How can I? I am at the end.

Sasha You're nowhere near the end.

Ivanov I've done it! I'm finished!

Sasha Keep your voice down! The guests . . .

Ivanov Finished!

Sasha We have to go to the church.

Ivanov The road I am on leads one way, and one way only. When a man who is educated, who is healthy – I'm by no means stupid – when a man like me starts on this path, then he's like a child wrapped in a blanket, who finds himself rolling downhill. What can stop me? What? I can't drink, wine gives me a headache. Write rotten poetry? I can't. I won't. I'm not willing to take my condition and somehow elevate it into something poetic. If I do that it's the end. I've always known the value of things. I call laziness laziness. The word for weakness is weakness. Oh, you say I'm not finished. I'm more finished than any man on earth.

He looks round.

We may be interrupted any moment. If you love me, do me one favour. Disown me. Disown me right now.

Sasha Oh Nikolai, if you had any idea how hard you make things.

Ivanov Analyse! Try to understand!

Sasha You're a kind man, a decent man. But every day you invent some terrible new task.

Ivanov You're not in love with me. You're in love with an idea. You set yourself the task of saving me. The idea of resurrection, that's what you love.

Sasha No!

Ivanov Every nerve in your body tells you to abandon me. Your body is screaming: let go of him. But it's your pride that prevents you.

Sasha It isn't true.

Ivanov How can you love me? Nobody could love me. This isn't love, it's stubbornness.

Sasha How can I walk away and leave you alone? How can I leave a man who has nothing? No family, no friends. Your estate is ruined, your money is gone. Everyone slanders you . . .

Ivanov I should never have come here. I should have stuck to my plan.

9

Lebedev *comes in, and at once* **Sasha** *runs over to him.*

Sasha Oh, Father, please help! Nikolai rushed in screaming like a lunatic, begging me to be kind, and call the wedding off.

Lebedev Kindness?

Ivanov There will be no wedding.

Sasha There will. Papa, tell him I know what I'm doing.

Lebedev Hold on, wait a moment. Why do you not want the wedding?

Ivanov I've explained to Sasha. She refuses to see.

Lebedev Don't tell her. Tell me. And do it in a way which makes sense. Really, Nikolai Alekseyevich, may God forgive you for this. You have brought more confusion into our lives than I ever dreamed possible. I feel I'm living in the skull of a demented skunk. What is the point? What do you want from me? That I challenge you to a duel?

Ivanov There's no need for a duel. I have said what I have to say, and in simple sentences.

Sasha *is walking up and down, distressed.*

Sasha This is terrible. He's become like a child.

Lebedev What am I meant to do? Throw up my hands in despair? Listen, Nikolai, no doubt to you, with all your new-fangled psychology what you're saying makes perfect sense. But to me it seems much the same as bad behaviour. Because life is actually quite simple. It is. The ceiling is white. Shoes are black. Sugar is sweet. You are in love with Sasha. She is in love with you. If you are still in love, stay. If you no longer love her, go. We won't hold it against you. You are both healthy, you are both intelligent, you have reasonable morals, a roof over your head and clothes on your back. What more do you need? Perhaps you need money. Of course. Money isn't everything, but on the other hand it's something. Your estate is mortgaged, I know that, and you have nothing to pay interest with. But I'm a father. I understand. Just for a moment leave your mother out of this, damn her. If she won't give you any more, so be it. Sasha says she doesn't want a dowry, fair enough. Principles, feminism, Schopenhauer – all that stuff. But I have ten thousand in the bank.

He looks around.

There's not a human being alive who knows this. Up till now. It belonged to your grandmother. Take it. It's for both of you. Only, if you could do me one small favour, can you give Shabyelski, I don't know, two thousand, say?

The guests are now gathering in the ballroom.

Ivanov Pasha, this is not about money. This is about conscience.

Sasha And I have a conscience too. You may talk all you wish but nothing will change. I am going to marry you. I refuse to let you go.

10

Sasha *goes out.*

Lebedev Nothing makes sense to me.

Ivanov Oh my poor friend, if only I could explain. If only I could say who I am. Honest, dishonest. Healthy, sick. Courageous, cowardly. I don't think I could ever put it into words. I was young, that's all. That's the only way to put it. I was full of faith, I believed. So few people bother. I worked and loved and tried and hoped and gave, all in full measure, without even measuring, never stopping to think: am I giving too much? Oh my dear Pasha, there are so few of us, so very few. So few of us and so much work to be done! And for this . . . arrogance, life has broken me. I am in my thirties, and already I am spending my days in a dressing-gown. With a heavy head and a sluggish soul. Exhausted, broken, cracked. Without belief, without love, without hope. Like a ghost I stagger among people, without knowing who I am or why I'm alive. In love I find no tenderness. In work I find no relief. In song I hear no music, in speeches I hear nothing new. Everywhere I go I feel revulsion for life. Inside I have died. Before you stands a man beaten at thirty-five, crushed by his own weakness and burnt out with his shame. All I have left, the thing that burns, that never stops burning, is the shame, the shame that turns now to anger.

He begins to sway.

I'm leaving my own self. What's happening? I can't even stand. Get Shabyelski. I have to go home.

11

From the drawing-room, voices are heard saying 'The best man's arrived.' **Shabyelski** *comes in.*

Shabyelski I'm coming. Dressed in an old tail-coat, of course. And without gloves. So all the sniggering has started, all the spiteful little jokes. What vermin they all are!

Borkin *comes in quickly with a bouquet. He is wearing tails and has a best man's buttonhole.*

Borkin Ay-ay-ay-ay! Where is the foolish fellow? Everyone's been waiting at the church for hours and here you are, philosophizing as usual, by the look of it. The man is a card. What a card he is! You're not meant to travel with the bride, remember? It's against the rules. You travel with me. Is that really too hard to grasp? The man is an irrepressible comedian.

Lvov *comes in and addresses* **Ivanov**.

Lvov Ah, you are here.

He speaks deliberately loudly.

Nikolai Alekseyevich, I am here to declare publicly that you are a scoundrel and a rogue.

Ivanov (*cold*) I thank you. From the bottom of my heart.

Now there is general astonishment. People are pouring into the room.

Borkin I have to say to you, sir, that you have insulted my friend. I challenge you to a duel.

Lvov Monsieur Borkin, I would find it degrading even to speak to you, let alone fight you. But your friend may have satisfaction whenever he likes.

Shabyelski I will fight you, sir. Yes, Count Shabyelski will fight!

Sasha (*to* **Lvov**) What is this? What happened? Did you challenge him?

Lvov I promise you, Alexandra Pavlovna, I did not challenge him without good reason. It is why I am here. I came today as an honest man to open your eyes. I ask you to listen to what I have to say.

Sasha What can you say? What is your news? That you are an honest man? That will hardly come as a revelation. On the contrary, Doctor Lvov, you have hounded us all with your so-called honesty. For weeks now, for months, you have pursued Ivanov, you have followed him like a shadow, you have interfered in his private life, you have slandered and judged him, and at every turn you have bombarded me and all his friends with anonymous letters. Yes! And all this in the guise of an honest man. Honest? Honest, was it, not even to spare his wife, never to let her rest, constantly to feed her suspicions, when she was dying. To feed her worst fears? And no doubt, it's clear, whatever you do in the future – be it murder or cruelty or just another act of downright mean-mindedness – they will all be excused. Why? Because you are an honest and enlightened young man.

Ivanov (*laughing*) Bravo! Not a wedding, a parliament! Bravo, bravo!

Sasha (*to* **Lvov**) Just think it over. Do you have any idea what you've done? Do you? You stupid, heartless people!

She takes **Ivanov** *by the hand.*

Let's get out of here, Nikolai. Come with us, Papa.

Ivanov Where can we go? Tell me. Where on earth can we go? I begin to see now, I begin to hear my young voice. My youth! The old Ivanov is stirring again.

He takes out a revolver.

Sasha I know what he's going to do. Stop him! Nikolai, for God's sake.

Ivanov I've gone down far enough. It's enough. Time to get out of here, yes. Thank you, Sasha. Time to go.

Sasha Nikolai, for God's sake! Stop him! Stop him!

Ivanov Let me free!

He runs to one side and shoots himself.

KING ALFRED'S COLLEGE
LIBRARY

also available

announcing the new Methuen Contemporary Dramatists *series*

Peter Barnes Plays: One
Peter Barnes Plays: Two
Peter Barnes Plays: Three

Howard Brenton Plays: One
Howard Brenton Plays: Two

Jim Cartright Plays: One

Caryl Churchill Plays: One
Caryl Churchill Plays: Two

David Mamet Plays: One
David Mamet Plays: Two
David Mamet Plays: Three

Willy Russell Plays: One

Sam Shepard Plays: One
Sam Shepard Plays: Three

Sue Townsend Plays: One

Methuen Modern Plays

include work by

Jean Anouilh
John Arden
Margaretta D'Arcy
Peter Barnes
Sebastian Barry
Brendan Behan
Edward Bond
Bertolt Brecht
Howard Brenton
Simon Burke
Jim Cartwright
Caryl Churchill
Noël Coward
Sarah Daniels
Nick Dear
Shelagh Delaney
David Edgar
Dario Fo
Michael Frayn
John Godber
Paul Godfrey
John Guare
Peter Handke
Jonathan Harvey
Iain Heggie
Declan Hughes
Terry Johnson
Barrie Keeffe
Stephen Lowe
Doug Lucie
John McGrath
David Mamet
Patrick Marber
Arthur Miller
Mtwa, Ngema & Simon
Tom Murphy
Phyllis Nagy
Peter Nichols
Joseph O'Connor
Joe Orton
Louise Page
Joe Penhall
Luigi Pirandello
Stephen Poliakoff
Franca Rame
Philip Ridley
Reginald Rose
David Rudkin
Willy Russell
Jean-Paul Sartre
Sam Shepard
Wole Soyinka
C. P. Taylor
Theatre de Complicite
Theatre Workshop
Sue Townsend
Judy Upton
Timberlake Wertenbaker
Victoria Wood

Methuen World Classics

Aeschylus (two volumes)
Jean Anouilh
John Arden (two volumes)
Arden & D'Arcy
Aristophanes (two volumes)
Aristophanes & Menander
Brendan Behan
Aphra Behn
Edward Bond (four volumes)
Bertolt Brecht
(five volumes)
Büchner
Bulgakov
Calderón
Anton Chekhov
Noël Coward (five volumes)
Sarah Daniels (two volumes)
Eduardo De Filippo
David Edgar (three volumes)
Euripides (three volumes)
Dario Fo (two volumes)
Michael Frayn (two volumes)
Max Frisch
Gorky
Harley Granville Barker
(two volumes)
Henrik Ibsen (six volumes)
Terry Johnson
Lorca (three volumes)
Marivaux
Mustapha Matura
David Mercer (two volumes)
Arthur Miller
(five volumes)
Anthony Minghella
Molière
Tom Murphy
(three volumes)
Musset
Peter Nichols (two volumes)
Clifford Odets
Joe Orton
Louise Page
A. W. Pinero
Luigi Pirandello
Stephen Poliakoff
(two volumes)
Terence Rattigan
Ntozake Shange
Sophocles (two volumes)
Wole Soyinka
David Storey (two volumes)
August Strindberg
(three volumes)
J. M. Synge
Ramón del Valle-Inclán
Frank Wedekind
Oscar Wilde

Methuen Student Editions

John Arden	*Serjeant Musgrave's Dance*
Alan Ayckbourn	*Confusions*
Aphra Behn	*The Rover*
Edward Bond	*Lear*
Bertolt Brecht	*The Caucasian Chalk Circle*
	Life of Galileo
	Mother Courage and her Children
Anton Chekhov	*The Cherry Orchard*
Caryl Churchill	*Top Girls*
Shelagh Delaney	*A Taste of Honey*
John Galsworthy	*Strife*
Robert Holman	*Across Oka*
Henrik Ibsen	*A Doll's House*
Charlotte Keatley	*My Mother Said I Never Should*
John Marston	*The Malcontent*
Willy Russell	*Blood Brothers*
August Strindberg	*The Father*
J. M. Synge	*The Playboy of the Western World*
Oscar Wilde	*The Importance of Being Earnest*
Tennessee Williams	*A Streetcar Named Desire*
Timberlake Wertenbaker	*Our Country's Good*

KING ALFRED'S COLLEGE
LIBRARY

new and forthcoming titles in the Methuen Film series

Beautiful Thing
Jonathan Harvey

The Crucible
Arthur Miller

The English Patient
Anthony Minghella

The Krays
Philip Ridley

Persuasion
Nick Dear after Jane Austen

The Reflecting Skin & The Passion of Darkly Noon
Philip Ridley

Twelfth Night
Trevor Nunn after Shakespeare